BETTER REGULATIONS
BETTER AI RESULTS

The Overlooked Policy Framework Governments and Policymakers Need to Regulate an AI-Driven World

ALFREDO GONZÁLEZ BRISEÑO

Better Regulations, Better AI Results

Copyright © 2026 by Alfredo González Briseño

Paperback ISBN: 978-1-963732-33-7
Hardback ISBN: 978-1-963732-35-1

Published by
The Publishing Pad
www.thepublishingpad.com

To Mariana and Sofia for being everything and enough.

To Tecuixpo, my sunshine. I fell in love with you
from the first moment I saw you.

To the present, the only and best place to live.

Praise for *Better Regulations, Better AI Results*

"*Better Regulations, Better AI Results* by Alfredo González Briseño offers a timely and practical guide to one of the defining challenges of our era: governing artificial intelligence while enabling innovation. Drawing on real-world policy experience, the book provides a clear framework for designing, implementing, and continuously improving AI regulation. Its emphasis on regulatory agility, institutional design, and leadership mindset is especially relevant in today's rapidly evolving landscape. A compelling and actionable resource for policymakers, industry leaders, and those shaping the future of AI governance."

—Bruce Huang, Ph.D., Ed.D.
Director, Master's Degree Program in Data Science and AI, Harvard Extension School
Affiliated Faculty, The Institute for Quantitative Social Science, Harvard University

Table of Contents

Introduction

The new wave of technological innovation is here. Well, to be fair, it has been around for some time. The difference is that Artificial Intelligence (AI) is mainstreaming rapidly across many social and economic activities. AI is now part of a new normal that touches your life, and there is no way back.

Some consider this watershed moment as important as the creation of electricity or the steam engine. As a consequence, everyone keeps talking about AI, its potential and how it will transform everything. If you are using AI, you understand this historical shift.

Governments and leaders worldwide are reacting by creating strategies and action plans to fully take advantage of this innovation. It is an *I-better-jump-on-the-bandwagon decision. Otherwise, my country or organization risks being left behind—way behind.*

So, we hear calls to regulate AI, arguing that it is too important to be overlooked and not regulated. These expressions have come not only from government leaders, academia and activists, but also from key actors in the AI industry.

As it always happens with disruptive technologies, regulation is now part of the conversation.

At the same time, there are calls to avoid stifling AI innovation with unnecessary rules. Lately, this demand has come to resemble a call to "stay out of the way." This was evident during the 2025 AI Action Summit in Paris, and what has followed in some countries. During the 2026 Summit in India, discussions turned towards having a unified global framework for AI governance.

If you are in government or leadership, it does not matter where you stand. You can be with those advocating for more regulation, with the opposite band demanding fewer restrictions—current and future—or perhaps somewhere in a "balanced" middle.

Regardless of your position, you need to know something important: *entering the AI space without a regulatory plan is planning for failure.*

In this book, my aim is not to talk about the specifics of one AI regulation or another. Yes, in Part 2, I will present a selection of key "what" issues in AI that you, as a leader in government or within your organization, need to be aware of, examine closely and decide whether to regulate.

That part of the book touches on different policy decisions to promote AI or protect us from AI. But, as I will say multiple times in this book, you must remember that regulation should always respond to context-specific and real problems or public policy objectives, not to perceptions.

My main goal in writing this book is to provide a quick overview of key strategic considerations when considering AI regulation.

You do not need to be an expert in regulation or AI, nor do you need to spend weeks reading this book. After a long flight, a weekend or even a single long night, you will gain a different perspective about AI regulation that very few in the world have.

For several years, I have advised governments around the globe on how to improve business regulations through public policy, technology and open government principles.

My field of work is not exactly rocket science. Yet, I know very few people in government and leadership who fully understand and, if they do, are willing to walk the talk of the overlooked policy that holds the key to helping them regulate an AI-driven world.

I am also an engineer who is still trying to solve problems with solutions that both integrate different parts while remaining simple and easy to grasp—so others can follow, if they decide to.

With that in mind, I did my best to present things clearly and in simple language throughout the book. By doing so, I hope to help you become better prepared, from a strategic perspective, to achieve better results with AI in your organization or country.

You might not find all the answers you are looking for here. It will be too pretentious of me to offer you that. However, I am sure you will find a few different answers and ideas to what you have heard before.

Some of the elements and concepts presented in this book are intended to nudge you toward a more proactive approach to regulating AI and future technological innovations, so, you can take action before issues explode right into your face or at least know how to respond more effectively.

In Part 1, I introduce simple concepts and ideas that will help you understand how to regulate better, including in the context of AI. The foundation of the three chapters in this first section comes from what many countries and international organizations refer to as better regulation, good regulatory practices, regulatory policy or governance, among others.

In Part 2, I zoom in on the "how" and the "what" of AI regulation. I make an important distinction between tools that boost and promote AI's growth, and regulatory solutions designed to protect people and the environment, as AI continues to scale and mainstream. This section concludes with a chapter on how AI itself can play an important role in improving regulation, including the regulation of AI.

Part 3 walks you through a series of reality-check considerations. These are issues you need to address in your government or organization to make things happen. These are key constraints that, for many years, have prevented governments and business leaders from getting regulation right. Without addressing them, it is very likely that the same problems will persist in the regulation of AI and future innovations.

At the end of Part 3, I introduce the *BRAIn Canvas,* a simple, strategic diagnostic tool for identifying the building blocks and gaps in AI regulation in your country or organization. It is designed to support the development of your government or business strategy in this space, so you know where and how to move forward.

Finally, in Part 4, I show you that this agenda goes far beyond AI regulation. If you are serious about it and recognize the possibilities ahead, you will be well positioned to transform your government, organization and country in a positive and responsible way.

However, as you will see in the final chapter, none of this will be possible without the transformation that matters most, the only transformation fully under your control. I am talking about your personal transformation.

This includes a shift in mindset. I introduce the ideas of "regulatory humility" and "positive coordination," which make possible the collaboration required among all stakeholders affected or interested in AI regulation. This is your best way to make change happen. These themes are explored in the book's last chapter, followed by a summary of key takeaways and a call to action.

I want to close this introduction by saying that there are many parallelisms between regulation and AI. Regulation has expanded to the point of becoming ubiquitous, touching every aspect of our daily lives. AI is now in the process of becoming something like that.

From a leadership point of view, dealing with regulation, in general, and AI should not be very different. Both are cross-sectoral issues that require action and coordination from every corner in the public sector.

Although not easy, getting AI regulation right should be simple, but governments and leaders are far from being like that, maybe because many people in leadership do not want or know how to keep things simple.

This book is for you, current or future government leader and decision-maker. This is for you who want to learn how to keep AI regulation simple. This is for you who want to drive positive and meaningful change in your country and organization, and prove to others that with better regulations, it is possible to get better AI results.

Key messages to remember

- Trying to enter the space of AI without a regulatory plan is planning for failure.
- This book is not about the details or content of specific AI regulations.
- Regulations should always respond to context-specific and real problems or public policy objectives.
- You do not need to be an expert on regulation or AI to read this book. My goal is to provide you with a quick, strategic overview of what you need to be aware of as a government or organization leader—current or future.

Part I

Learning to Regulate Better

Before running, your organization or government needs to learn how to walk first. Better AI regulation begins with becoming a better regulator. If you are not there yet, AI regulation is a great place to start or to build on existing foundations.

In this first part of the book, I explore the underlying dynamics between technological innovation and regulation. I also examine the different objectives that government-made rules serve—some of which go beyond promoting innovation alone.

Here, I introduce the public policy approach that many governments and business leaders have overlooked or dismissed for years, despite its potential to improve regulatory outcomes. I describe this policy in detail and explain why it matters now more than ever.

Beyond the Pacing Problem

"I am not an advocate for frequent changes in laws and constitutions, but laws and institutions must go hand in hand with the progress of the human mind. As that becomes more developed, more enlightened, as new discoveries are made, new truths discovered and manners and opinions change, with the change of circumstances, institutions must advance also to keep pace with the times."

—Thomas Jefferson[1]

What Do You Mean by Pacing Problem?

It works like a perpetual cycle. Technological innovation erupts onto the scene, breaking established schemes in social and economic life. Governments, regulators and business leaders are usually not ready to accommodate new circumstances, so they try to catch up.

---

1   Letter from Thomas Jefferson to Samuel Kercheval, July 12, 1816; Library of Congress. This quote appears also as an inscription on the southeast wall of the Thomas Jefferson Memorial in Washington, D.C., to represent his views on government.

A few times, they come up with decent rules and frameworks. More often, they act—or react—ineffectively. The outcome is a combination of poor results and still staying behind.

Welcome to the world of the pacing problem of regulation.[1]

To some extent, this perpetual cycle is natural and inevitable. Regulation will always be behind innovation.

Why? Because disruptive technologies are, like their name says, disruptive in nature. Nobody—except their creators—sees them coming. Let alone foresee their consequences.

Also, innovation is driven by profit-oriented companies. In a market economy, businesses often seek more and move rapidly. Governments and regulators, as you know, do not function and move at the same pace.

An article by the World Economic Forum (WEF) presents this dynamic clearly:

"It can take weeks to introduce a new idea or business model but years to pass a change in the law."[2]

But there is also a fundamental issue I mentioned in the introduction that you should not forget. Good regulation responds only to specific problems and policy objectives, not general ideas or perceptions.

This implies that it is not the best plan to think, or even act, guided by the perception of "let's regulate this because it seems important or troublesome." The definition of "what" you are going to regulate and "why" is extremely important.

Humanity has been through several waves of technological innovation. The current challenge is that those waves are coming more frequently.

Not even 10 years ago, sharing economy platforms were part of the conversation. Then, we had crypto. Now we have AI and Gen AI. Self-driving cars will start to become mainstream. In a not-so-distant future, we will have AI-powered humanoid robots.

The point is that addressing the pacing problem will not become easier. Quite the opposite.

There is, of course, an expectation for governments and policy makers to be ready, better prepared and in the driver's seat. Yes, regulation will always be behind. But that does not mean that it should be a thousand miles behind innovation.

The Call for Agile Governments and Regulation

So, waves of disruptive technologies like AI are hitting you straight in the face. You have barely recovered when the next one is ready to pound you down again.

You know you have to do something about it. You are "The Government" or "The Leader," and need to be better prepared. Practitioners, experts and other stakeholders are expecting you to step up and rise to the occasion. Although many in the industry will use their power to influence your AI rules, they also know everyone will benefit if you get AI regulation right.

For years, this expectation has been framed as what some institutions and experts call "agile regulation." It is a solution to address the pacing problem.

As its name directly implies, the objective is for governments to be more agile. In theory, it means adapting policies and rules to respond quickly to the changing and evolving social and market conditions.[3]

Agile regulation is at the essence of Thomas Jefferson's quote at the beginning of this chapter. The big difference is that now we may need a more iterative process than what Jefferson had in mind centuries ago. But agile government and regulation seem to be part of his vision as a Founding Father.

While it is commonly talked about, there is no formal or globally agreed-upon definition of agile regulation. A good international reference is the Organisation for Economic Co-operation and Development (OECD). It has a "Practical Guidance on Agile Regulatory Governance to Harness Innovation," developed by its Regulatory Policy Council.

In this practical guidance, the OECD shares recommendations for countries to adapt their regulatory management tools to make sure their regulations are fit for purpose.[4] In other words, to make sure they remain relevant to current realities.

Some aspects of AI regulation that I present and propose in this book resonate, to some extent, with recommendations from the OECD and other international organizations.

However, this only gives you a framework. It becomes useful only when you take this advice to your country or organization and implement something that balances good international recommendations with what fits and makes sense for your local goals and context.

In 2023, the United Kingdom (the UK) took similar measures to address issues in AI regulation. The government launched "A pro-innovation approach to AI regulation."[5]

This country framework, with five principles, provided guidance on the responsible development and use of AI in the British economy. The purpose was to bring clarity and coherence to the field of AI regulation.

It Is More Than a Pacing Issue

More countries are following the UK. Many governments have already incorporated agility or similar concepts into their public speech, especially with the growing popularity of AI. In part, it is to show that they know what needs to be done. That they are on top of things. But at some point, you need to begin to practice what you preach to get better results. You need to walk the talk.

This is where reality shows that, despite good intentions, many governments continue to simply not be agile. They are still trying to catch up with innovation, including AI. They are being left behind—way behind.

After several years of working on regulatory issues and witnessing how governments deal with regulation, something became clear. The pacing problem is not only about regulating AI and other technological innovations. As a government or business leader, you are certainly aware of this.

If you are a future leader, you need to know this:

The pacing problem is more about poor regulatory practices trying to catch up and become good regulatory practices that will lead to better policy results, including in the field of AI.

In other words, the big deal lies in the capacity or incapacity of governments and leaders to regulate well. So, let's stop for a moment and think about the specific challenge of regulating AI.

Overall, governments and leaders with a strong track record and better capacity to regulate effectively are better positioned to get AI regulation right and achieve better results from this technological innovation.

Conversely, if governments or leaders are not really good at regulation, it is highly likely that they will struggle to regulate AI well.

This also tells us that it will be extremely rare to find governments and organizations that are not good at regulation and struggle with it to suddenly excel at AI regulation.

So, what is the lesson that you take from this? What do you think you have to do first to get AI regulation right?

Food for Thought on What Goes First

If you agree that "you have to learn to walk before you can run," many parts of this book will guide you, from a strategic perspective, on things you need to do before you can run and pull off AI regulation.

Of course, time is of the essence. Remember, the waves are hitting you in the face and pounding you down over and over.

So, before we move on, I want to leave you with some food for thought about the popular discussions of the pacing problem and calls for regulation not to kill innovations like AI.

Keeping up with innovation is not an end in itself for regulation. Especially when desirable public goods are at risk.

Failing to react quickly is not always a complete failure if you agree that, in many cases, governments and leaders should not rush regulatory decisions.

Regulatory failures often stem from poorly planned, analyzed and socialized changes in government-made rules. Thus, balancing a government's capacity for agility and adaptability in rulemaking while protecting the public good is an issue that goes beyond the regulation of technological innovation and lies at the core of regulation in any field.

Key messages to remember

- Regulation will always be behind innovation. However, it does not have to be a thousand miles behind.
- The real pacing problem is not about regulation catching up with AI and other innovations. It is about poor regulatory practices trying to catch up to become good regulatory practices that deliver better policy results.
- Keeping up with innovation is not the main purpose of regulation. Especially when desirable public goods in your country or organization are at risk.

2

Regulation and Its Purposes

"Institutions are the rules of the game in a society or, more formally, are the humanly devised constraints that shape human interaction... Institutions reduce uncertainty by providing a structure to everyday life. They are a guide to human interaction..."

—Douglass North

"If we want our regulators to do better, we have to embrace a simple idea: regulation isn't an obstacle to thriving free markets; it's a vital part of them."

—James Surowiecki

In the previous chapter, we discussed the pacing problem, in which regulation is always behind innovation, and trying to catch up with it. Before we continue, it is important to take a step back and understand regulation as the policy tool many want to apply to or remove from the path of AI and future innovations.

Let's talk about regulation, its essence and main purposes.

My first conceptual understanding of rules like regulations came from an economics perspective. I was in my early professional years at IPADE Business School in Mexico, when I became fascinated by Douglass North's idea of institutions, or as he calls them, "the rules of the game in society."

In brief, I will discuss how regulations are part of North's concept of the rules of the game. Before that, let me explain what I mean by "regulation" in this book.

My Definition of Regulation

You do not have to be a lawyer to know that there are government-made rules that are more important than others. As a government leader, you are very aware of this. Bear with me for a second while I elaborate briefly on this point for future leaders and other readers.

A country's constitution is often the main legal framework to which other rules must respond or align. You also have national laws that govern specific topics. Countries also have international and supranational agreements or treaties.

At some point, these norms high up in the legal hierarchy need to become more specific about their mandate. That is when other legal instruments, like regulations, come into play.

Regulations allow policymakers and rulemakers to get granular in the implementation of principles, obligations, restrictions and other commands that come from constitutions, national laws and international agreements, often the outcome of discussions and consensus at a higher political level. These high-level legal mandates trickle down into rules governing more specific policy domains and socioeconomic activities.

This general picture is important because it makes clear that regulation does not emerge spontaneously or come out of left field. On the contrary, all regulations should originate from and respond to a higher legal instrument, like the ones described above.

So, what comprises the universe of regulation? It varies by country. However, among the different regulatory instruments that countries use, you may find decrees—either presidential, ministerial or royal—executive orders or instructions, ministerial resolutions, technical regulations, national standards, sanitary and phytosanitary measures, guidelines, agreements and more.

It is important to clarify that all these government-made rules, which I will refer to as regulations, are created by the executive power. For the purpose of this book, I will leave out laws passed by the legislative power. These rules usually emanate from different procedures, discussions and agreements, setting principles and mandates that do not touch on the specifics of how public policies should be implemented.

I am also leaving out what some people classify as administrative acts or non-substantive regulation. These types of administrative regulations are used for appointing government officials, approving their travel or leave, or even nominating public awards. These decisions formalized through regulation do not always impose significant obligations on individuals, firms and organizations.

Another relevant feature to be aware of is that regulations come with requirements, obligations or guidelines. In principle, they often have consequences for non-compliance.

This last characteristic is important because, without consequences, repercussions, or at least a perceived threat of them, regulations lose an important part of their capacity to influence behavior.

However, there are other regulatory instruments that operate by creating adequate incentives, without necessarily imposing obligations or the threat of punishment for non-compliance.

Having all these aspects in mind, as part of a presentation I made a few years ago, I came up with the following definition:

Feel free to use or adjust this definition as a general framework to identify the instruments and tools that your government or leadership formally considers or uses as regulation, and that will most likely have an impact on AI.

North's Rules of the Game

This chapter started with a quote from Douglass North's book *Institutions, Institutional Change and Economic Performance.* I highly recommend that you read it, as well as North's other literature and writings.

Before we continue, you may ask who Douglass North is, and what he said that is relevant to regulation.

North is the winner of the 1993 Nobel Prize in Economic Science. He is famous, among other things, for his theory of institutions.

Many of us think of institutions as organizations or government bodies, such as the police, a ministry, the presidency, or the military. However, North's vision is very different.

He understands institutions as *"the rules of the game in a society or, more formally, as the humanly devised constraints that shape human interaction."*[6]

These constraints include a combination of what individuals [or firms] are prohibited from doing and what they are allowed to do under certain circumstances. Institutions, constraints or rules of the game come in many forms. According to North, they can be:

1. Formal rules of a political, judicial and economic nature, including constitutions, laws, regulations and contracts; and,

2. Informal rules, such as codes of conduct, norms of behavior and social conventions.

Therefore, *regulations are part of an organization's or a country's formal written rules of the game.*

However, you also need to be aware that informal rules matter. As a government or business leader, you know it. Unwritten rules influence and sometimes are more determinant than formal ones like regulations.

Having said that, the importance of institutions, including regulation, lies in the fact that, as North explains, they reduce uncertainty by providing a stable and less costly structure for everyday interactions and exchanges.

Have you heard the phrase *"a predictable regulatory environment"*? Well, this book is, in great part, about how to achieve that in AI regulation. North provides a very solid foundation for that discussion.

The rules of the game matter, too, because they create incentives that ultimately determine which economic activities are profitable and viable.

In North's words, institutions are *"the underlying determinant of the long-run performance of economies."*[7]

To close this section, it is important to note that "profitable and viable" economic activities do not always mean productive or efficient outcomes. As North warns, many countries are poor because their institutions incentivize political and economic actors to pursue unproductive activities. The cycle of inefficient results is perpetuated when these same actors influence how these institutions continue to evolve.

You need to be conscious of these dynamics, as they may enable—or prevent—your country and organization from reaping the benefits of AI.

It Is All About Public Policy Objectives

Let's bring the concept and purpose of regulation down to the things you do or will be doing in government or leadership.

In the literature and even in practice, you will often find that regulations are used to address and correct market failures. These may include monopolies, scarcity of goods, externalities like pollution or information asymmetries.

Yes, these are very valid reasons for regulation. However, they present the purpose of regulation as a remedy, trying to react to problems after they emerge.

It is just like the pacing problem discussed in the previous chapter. An issue comes up, then regulation is called upon to save the day, or at least to show that something has been done.

Instead of this reactive vision, I prefer to think about a more proactive one, in which regulation is understood as a steering wheel that governments and leaders use to move toward better results. By results, I mean public policy results.

From this perspective, regulation takes on a more interesting and strategic function.

If we view regulation as an instrument for achieving public policy objectives, we can understand the dual role of government-made rules in affecting businesses and industries such as AI.

On one hand, regulation can lead to better economic results by boosting productivity, investment, trade, innovation and growth. On the other hand, it can protect and defend desirable public goods, such as public health, consumer safety, labor conditions, the environment and natural resources, social benefits, education and others.

In Part 2, I will elaborate on this dual role: how regulation can enable AI's growth while protecting us from its unintended consequences and irresponsible use.

You are right if you think this can be complex and contradictory in many cases. But balancing these different policy objectives is what makes this field so interesting.

Of course, governments can achieve public policy goals through other means. They have public spending and taxes, including nowadays-popular tariffs. But as my friend and former colleague Peter Ladegaard once said, there is a limit to how much governments can spend, tax or impose tariffs. This is where regulation gains relevance.

The advantage, and often the terrifying part of it, is that regulations, including AI rules, can be easily created without huge investments of human or financial capital.

I use the word *terrifying* because, with the stroke of a pen, rules can be created in days, often without much clarity or reflection on their short- or long-term consequences.

We will dive into this issue in the next two chapters. For now, let's stay with the fact that regulations are created every single day to pursue public policy objectives. As a government or business leader, you probably understand me when I say "every single day."

How Much Is Enough?

Colombia and many other countries know this well. Regulatory production can be likened to cooking pancakes. It is so easy. One rule follows another until it becomes an issue known as "*regulatory inflation*."

This is something to consider as waves of new AI regulation are drafted.

So, let me ask you: What would you think is an ideal "amount" of regulation your country or a regular society should have?

This question deserves a separate line of research or an entire book. Even in pro-market economies, which you would assume prefer less market intervention, you usually hear calls for the government to regulate, especially when there is a perceived threat to the public good. Just like it is happening with some aspects of AI.

Usually, there are two extremes and many positions in between. On one side, you have those who like government intervention as a powerful ruler bringing order to almost everything.

On the other side, you find those who believe government power and scope of influence should be limited to the minimum necessary, usually just to protect people's natural rights.

Depending on where you find yourself and your government on this spectrum, at some point you will need to find a balance—as with most things in life.

Why does balance matter? Because regulation or lack of regulation comes with benefits and, more often, costs.

- Costs for citizens and businesses needing to comply with rules.
- Costs for government agencies that have to monitor and enforce compliance.
- Costs to the environment, consumer health, data privacy, and intellectual property, as we are seeing with AI, due to the absence of regulation.

When I worked in Malaysia with the World Bank, advising the Malaysia Productivity Corporation, I learned about PEMUDAH. It is a special task force that brings together the public and private sectors to improve the country's business environment.

Among PEMUDAH's values, you can find *"no more regulation than necessary."*

In its mission statement, PEMUDAH expresses the task force's role in *"creating a harmonious equilibrium between the necessity for regulatory governance and the timely and cost-effective implementation of business decisions and operations."*

I already said that regulation is ubiquitous, affecting and touching most of our daily lives and activities. AI is moving in the same direction.

In their book *The Behavioral Code: The Hidden Ways that Law Makes us Better… or Worse*, Van Rooij and Fine write about the code—legal code—we would be able to see if we took a hypothetical red pill, just like Neo did in the movie *The Matrix*. Both authors say, "*the red pill would reveal that laws and legal rules are omnipresent.*"[8]

Whether we see the code or not, when you enter the space of AI regulation, you should not get lost in whether more or less regulation is needed.

What matters is the "*harmonious equilibrium*" that PEMUDAH talks about. That is where regulation serves its purpose: achieving public policy objectives without unnecessarily interfering with or imposing burdens on citizens and firms.

Key messages to remember

- As North says, regulations are part of the formal rules of the game in society.
- They reduce uncertainty in everyday life's interactions and exchanges and are determinants of long-term economic performance.
- Regulations are also an important tool to achieve policy objectives, including economic growth and development, and the protection and pursuit of desirable public goods.
- The conversation should not be whether more or less regulation is better. It should be about finding the balance that achieves the two objectives above.

The Overlooked Policy Holding the Key

"The process is everything, the outcome is nothing."

—Attributed to Bruce Lee

"Yes, results do matter. But if you optimize for the outcome, you win one time. If you optimize for a process that leads to great outcomes, you can win again and again."

—James Clear

The subtitle of this book reads *"The Overlooked Policy Framework Governments and Policymakers Need to Regulate an AI-Driven World."*

You may wonder what the overlooked policy the subtitle alludes to is. Well, you may have heard of it before. It has different names, depending on the context or who is talking about it.

The OECD refers to it as regulatory policy. In Europe, a common term is better regulation. In Latin America, it is translated as regulatory improvement. Within the field of international trade organizations, institutions and agreements, the common name is Good Regulatory Practices or GRP. At some point during my career at the World Bank, we called it regulatory governance or regulatory management.

I like GRP and better regulation because of what both names transmit from a communications perspective. They have a positive message and words that are difficult to say no to when you present it to governments and other audiences. Nonetheless, lately I have been using regulatory policy.

Why regulatory policy? Mainly because this name gives explicit recognition and status of public policy to this domain.

This matters because it is difficult to rationally conceive a public policy without an adequate institution, mandate and resources (human and financial) for its successful implementation. In the context of AI regulation, I will discuss these last issues in Part 3 of the book.

The Building Blocks of Regulatory Policy

Because regulatory policy has a strong influence on getting AI regulation right, let's cut to the chase and discuss upfront its essence. Then, we can take care of the details and context.

In a nutshell, a sound or useful regulatory policy implies having in place:

1. a government-wide policy,
2. an institution to lead and guide its implementation; and
3. a set of good regulatory practices to improve the process of how regulations are planned, designed, implemented and reviewed.

This is the gist of regulatory policy. Below, I present its key elements visually and elaborate on them. Of course, every country implements this framework differently. So, let's go over some of the practical nuances you will find in the world, including your country.

Key Elements of a Regulatory Policy

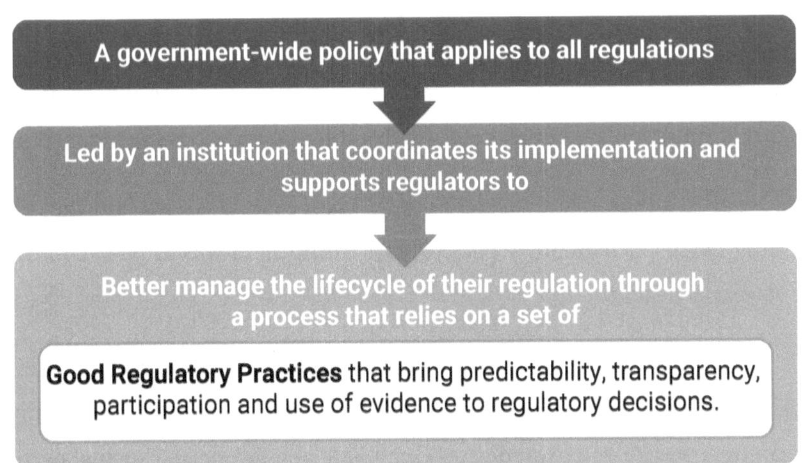

First, a government-wide policy that applies to "all regulations" is often an unattainable desirable goal. If you want to have better regulations—including AI regulations—with the help of regulatory policy, you will have to apply its principles, tools and requirements to all rules in your country's regulatory environment. Otherwise, the overall effect becomes diluted.

In practice, most countries find this very difficult to achieve. They have independent regulators operating under their own specific mandates. They have subnational governments, which display poor coordination with their national counterparts. Finally, you have reluctance from governments dipping their toes in this public policy, without fully committing in the short term—or ever at all—to its principles and whole-of-government approach.

One of my messages to you in this book is not to encourage you as a government or business leader to go for the whole shebang of a government-wide regulatory policy.

If your country or organization has done it or is in the process of doing it, that's great and wonderful. If regulatory policy is simply nonexistent or in its infancy in your country/business, here is what I propose to you:

Use AI regulation as a niche and excuse to put into practice all regulatory policy lessons and resources to improve rules, in this case, government-made rules affecting AI.

Some countries have done it, for instance, with trade-related regulation. It is an important subset of government rules with strong implications for the economy.

Because of AI's high relevance, let's take it as an example to explain the other building blocks of regulatory policy. Start thinking of this as your country's "AI Regulatory Policy."

This policy could be drafted simply as a standalone policy document or even backed by a legal instrument like a national law, a presidential decree, a council of ministers' decree or a royal decree. But before you decide on the final output, you need to know what should be included in it.

You will need an institution that leads and coordinates AI regulation across government. The coordination part is extremely important. Agricultural, environmental and other sectoral regulations are always overseen by a designated ministry or government department. But AI is cross-sectoral. It touches many areas within government.

That is why coordination of AI regulation is important. Chapter 9 will go deeper into this. For the moment, I invite you to reflect on the type of institution or agency within your country's public administration that is best suited for this role.

There are many possibilities, and there is no single right or wrong solution. You can consider creating a new AI agency with a mandate to oversee AI regulation across the government and leadership. You can also think of existing agencies within your government structure where this agenda could fit well.

This institution may or may not have AI regulatory powers. If that is the case, it will have more direct control over the regulation it creates. However, in every country and organization, other regulators will still need to address several aspects of AI within their respective domains.

Thus, another important function of the AI institution is to support other regulators in creating better AI regulations.

How can you do that? By helping regulatory agencies adopt Good Regulatory Practices (GRP). When applied consistently, GPR can bring predictability, transparency, participation and the use of evidence to regulatory decisions affecting AI.

Chapter 4 provides more details on this. For now, you need to understand that adopting GRP is part of a process. A different regulatory process than the one your country probably has or lacks.

This "regulatory process" will enable you to actively manage the lifecycle of AI regulations—from conception through analysis, drafting, consultation, approval, implementation, and simplification, until it is time to review results.

Because this process matters and influences the quality of the regulations your government produces, let's talk briefly about what that process looks like.

The Process Matters, Too!

There are many problems with regulation. However, there is one that lies at the core of the rest, and as a decision maker, you are likely aware of it.

It is like playing on a soccer team where all players want to be the star and score, and no one wants to sacrifice on defense, let alone be the goalie. A complete mess!

In this "lack of process," regulators in many countries tend to act with wide discretion, no guidance and weak capacity to design, draft and implement regulations within their domain. When this happens, regulations lose meaningful purpose, direction and impact.

To make things worse, the rationale for regulation usually responds only to orders that come from "above"— instructions from the president, prime minister, a sectoral minister or the head of an agency. In other cases, I have heard them say that they regulate simply because a primary law says they have to do it.

Now, you may start connecting the dots and seeing where this source problem leads to.

I already mentioned regulatory inflation. Because of poor management and oversight in issuing regulations, it is not rare to see that many governments do not know the exact number of regulations they have.

Another typical consequence is the accumulation of regulations that have endured over time. Some of which still exist on paper but are no longer applied. In the worst cases, rules are still implemented but are completely outdated.

Finally, a lack of process leads to many regulatory failures. They take the form of unnecessary regulatory burdens: contradictory or duplicative mandates from different government agencies, and flip-flopping or reversal of regulatory decisions, to name a few.

How do you fix this? What is the right process to replace the lack of process?

Instead of regulating at will, your *AI Regulatory Policy* requires that your AI institution, or similar agency leading AI across government, actively follow and oversee AI regulations in your country or organization—both new and existing.

As we said before, this starts with the rules being just an idea, before they are inked on paper. It continues through their design, drafting, publication, implementation, simplification, and closes the cycle with a final review to assess results and continued relevance. Let's call this: *The "how" of regulating AI.*

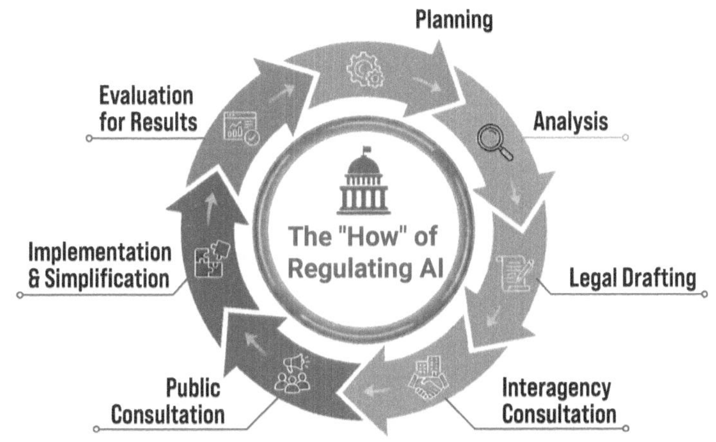

The objective of this process is to proactively manage the lifecycle of every regulation.

That is why regulatory policy is also called regulatory management or governance. Your AI agency's role is to coordinate and support other agencies in implementing this process.

For every single box in the process, there are Good Regulatory Practices (GRP) or tools and procedures that help governments and AI regulators make decisions that are more predictable, transparent, participatory and evidence-based.

This is all about the "how" to regulate, not the "what" to regulate. The next chapter will elaborate on this. For the moment, get familiar with the idea that "how" you regulate AI will matter equally or more than "what" you regulate about AI.

It is very rare to find a government that consistently applies this process to all its regulations. But, as we said, you do not have to go for the whole shebang. You just need to start applying this process to AI regulation.

So, It Matters, but Why?

We have discussed the consequences of a lack of process. But there is more to having and following an AI regulatory governance or management process.

You may have heard about the concept of regulatory quality. As abstract as this idea may sound, there is a broad consensus that the quality of regulations—individual and aggregate—impacts productivity, investment, international trade, innovation and overall economic performance.

The entire purpose of regulatory policy, or your AI version, is to improve the quality of regulations, including AI regulations. That is why regulatory policy is also called better regulation or regulatory improvement.

It is very valid if, at this point, you still ask, "What is regulatory quality? If that is the goal, how do I achieve it?"

While this is a daunting task, I will start with what the OECD has said over the years. A 2008 Policy Brief mentions that regulatory quality depends greatly on "*how regulations are conceived and made.*"[9]

In the glossary of a more recent publication, the OECD more specifically mentions:

"The notion of regulatory quality covers process, i.e., the way regulations are developed and enforced, which should follow the key principles of consultation, transparency, accountability and evidence-base. The notion of regulatory quality also covers outcomes, i.e., regulations that are effective at achieving their objectives, efficient, coherent and simple."[10]

This definition includes two key elements: the process we have discussed and the outcomes and results of the rules.

A common mistake is that, when we think about good regulation, we often focus on the text and content of that rule. Some governments focus most of their efforts on that milestone. However, the process leading to that regulation and the process used to implement it matter equally, and sometimes more than a technically perfect rule on paper.

I will close this chapter by saying there is more to it when we discuss the process. If you want to go deeper, I recommend the *"psychology of procedural justice."* Lind and Arndt are a great place to start.

For the moment, I will just say that the psychology of procedural justice, also called *"procedural fairness,"* touches precisely on the process or "how" regulations are designed and implemented.

In their literature, Lind and Arndt cite several studies showing that *"acceptance of rules, compliance with regulations and administrative decisions, and trust in government are all improved if regulatory processes incorporate elements that enhance perceived fairness."*[11]

It is simply beautiful what you can achieve through a fair process.

Let's move forward, so I can share a few strategic, quick lessons on "how" you can do it.

Key messages to remember

- A key driver of poor regulation is that governments regulate at will, without order, principles, common guidelines or standard procedures.

- Improving the quality of regulation requires improving the "how" of regulation. This "how" is often more important than "what" is regulated.

- A sound regulatory policy provides the necessary framework, institutions and tools to proactively manage regulations throughout their lifecycle.

- If your country or organization does not have a regulatory policy in place, start with AI regulation and create your "AI Regulatory Policy."

Part II

Better AI Regulation, "How" and "What" to Regulate

"How" your government regulates AI will matter more than "what" aspect of AI you regulate. This is a key lesson from the overlooked policy described in Part 1.

Here, in Part 2, I present a quick and strategic overview of the "how" of regulating AI. While this book does not intend to tell you the specifics of this or that AI regulation, I want to share a few "what" issues you need to be aware of.

Some of those "what" issues are about regulations or regulatory tools that can help promote AI in your country or organization. Balancing the equation, I will also highlight other "what" issues arising from the design and implementation of AI that may require regulatory solutions to protect people from unintended consequences and irresponsible use.

Finally, I will share ideas on how AI itself can help you regulate AI and other domains more effectively.

4

Quick Lessons on "How" to Regulate AI

"Failing to plan is planning to fail."

—Allen Lakein

"Take nothing on its looks; take everything on evidence. There's no better rule."

—Charles Dickens

"Fair treatment in the hearings, meetings and online consultations used to design regulations including possibilities for all interested parties to be heard provides a way to enhance acceptance of the rule-making process and of the regulations ultimately put forth."

—Lind and Arndt

Most of what we have discussed so far was an important prelude to Part 2, namely, "how" to regulate AI better.

What I present here matters for improving AI regulation, but you can also apply it to other regulatory domains.

As I said before, it will be very unusual to find a government excelling at AI regulation while performing poorly in all other regulatory areas.

Conversely, if your government has a strong track record of regulatory decision-making, you are better positioned to approach AI regulation more effectively.

Regardless of where you are today, remember that in addition to aiming for specific good AI regulations, you also need to keep an eye on improving the process that leads to those AI rules. So, do not forget about this process:

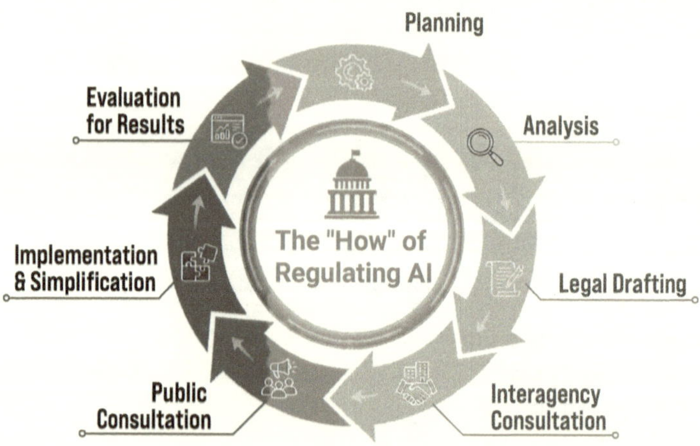

It is now time to get our hands a little wet and start exploring how your government and organization can adopt elements of this process to improve new and future AI regulation.

Everything Starts with Planning

Actually, everything should start with a problem. We will talk about that soon. But once you have decided to enter the space of regulatory solutions, as a path to finding possible answers to a public AI problem your country or organization is facing, the first thing you need to do is to plan.

By planning, I mean orderly planning for regulatory changes. These changes include the introduction of new regulations or the review of existing ones. This is highly relevant for AI regulation.

It may sound simple and logical, but believe me when I say that this is barely done well around the world.

As a leader, you know it. Decisions on regulatory changes are typically fast-tracked. A head of government, a minister or a senior official gives the order, *"We need this regulation now!"* Then, everything becomes a rushed dance to come up with the decree, resolution or rule in question as quickly as possible.

What is the problem with this? From a bureaucratic perspective, you are following orders and, in the process, saving your job by delivering what was requested. For the rest of us outside government and leadership, the result can be an absolute nightmare!

During my time at the World Bank, I traveled to different countries to advise governments on regulatory policy. However, a good practice was to always meet with the private sector. Businesses are a useful mirror in which regulation reflects its real gains and pains.

In many of those meetings, I heard members of business associations complain about what they called *"weekend regulations."*

When I asked what they meant, the description was a process in which regulatory changes were announced on Friday and came into effect on Monday.

You do not have to be Einstein to understand that this way of making decisions takes everyone by surprise. It leaves no space for reactions and feedback from those affected by AI regulatory changes.

Acting like this leaves behind one of the most important things treasured by investors, entrepreneurs or anyone considering doing business in your country: *"regulatory predictability."*

The reasons you should care about regulatory predictability are self-explanatory. However, let me quickly share some evidence on this.

The World Bank, in its latest Global Investment Competitiveness (GIC) Report, highlights this point. The 2019 GIC Survey behind the report's data shows that nearly 9 out of 10 investors consider political stability, macroeconomic stability and a country's legal and regulatory environment to be "important" or "critically important" for investment decisions.[12]

These were the top three reported factors for foreign investment decisions. Not fiscal incentives, market size or cheap labor.

Nearly two-thirds of the GIC survey respondents also highlighted the importance of policy predictability and confidence for global investment decisions.

So, what are the implications for AI regulation?

First, you need to remember that *"predictability starts with good planning."* Here, I am talking about regulatory planning.

One way to achieve this is through a Good Regulatory Practice (remember GRP?) that some countries call "forward regulatory plans," "regulatory plans," or simply "regulatory agenda."

You may be surprised by how easy it can be for your government/leadership to adopt an AI regulatory plan. Let's get into the details of its "what" and "why."

The bare-bones version of an AI regulatory plan is this: *a publicly available list announcing each AI regulation that will be introduced or changed in the near future, within the next 6, 12, or 24 months.*

Two elements to highlight from this description are that the plan is "publicly available", and that the announcement should be released in advance, between 6–24 months before AI regulatory changes take effect.

Together, these elements bring transparency, access to information, advanced notice, and—you guessed it—predictability about regulatory changes.

To get the most out of it, the practical implementation of your AI regulatory plan should go beyond a simple list with names of rules to be amended. Canada is a very good reference point for thinking about what your AI regulatory plan could include. The box below shows how they do it.

Forward Regulatory Plans in Canada

Canada's Policy on Regulatory Transparency and Accountability provides specific details on how federal agencies should implement forward regulatory plans.[13] Regarding the substance or content of each regulatory plan, the Policy requires the following description in simple language for every regulation in the forward plan:

1. Working title of the regulatory initiative, reflecting the nature and subject of the proposed change.
2. Enabling acts, which give authority for the proposed initiative.
3. A description of the initiative and its objectives.
4. Potential impact on Canadians, including businesses. This section should identify stakeholder groups or sectors affected by the proposal, as well as expected impacts on international trade or investment.
5. Regulatory cooperation efforts (domestic and international).
6. Consultations, including a description of past consultations as well as details about planned and upcoming consultations with stakeholders.

7. Further information on data, research and analysis that support the initiative.

8. Departmental contact information.

9. The date the regulatory initiative was first included in the Forward Regulatory Plan.

Source: Canada's Cabinet Directive on Regulation and the Federal Government's Policy on Regulatory Transparency and Accountability.

Of course, how you adapt or implement this tool in your country or organization is crucial. However, no matter what details you decide to include in your AI regulatory plans, remember that—although they might look simple and inconsequential—they create a solid foundation for regulatory predictability and for the next steps in your AI regulatory process.

Key messages to remember

- Regulatory predictability is very important. It starts with planning and announcing upcoming regulatory changes.
- A regulatory plan is a publicly available list that provides enough details about regulatory changes in the next 6–24 months.
- Implement an AI regulatory plan for upcoming changes to AI regulations. It is a solid place to start.

Identify the Problem and Question Regulation as the Best Solution

The AI regulatory process starts with planning. But every AI regulatory decision should originate from a public policy problem. A real and tangible problem.

This is why it is not very useful when someone says that AI should be regulated without elaborating on the why.

For example, in May 2023, Google's CEO said, "I still believe AI is too important not to regulate and too important not to regulate well."[14]

Similar statements have been shared by other big players in the AI industry and, of course, governments and leaders worldwide. However, calls like this tend to leave out the specific problems AI regulation or deregulation are meant to solve.

In theory, the idea that everything should start with a problem sounds great. In practice, however, regulatory decisions do not follow this logic. That is not how government typically works, right? So, what can you do?

First, you need to work this out through your AI regulatory plan. When you design it, include a line item requiring regulators to state the problem they are trying to address with their planned regulation.

If you cannot do this, because you have not yet implemented an AI regulatory plan, there is plan B. This alternative requires that you use a GRP called *"ex ante regulatory impact analysis,"* commonly known as RIA. We will call it *"AI RIA."*

Before we dive into what AI RIA is, let's briefly discuss why you should bother to do it.

In a nutshell, the essence of any RIA is to provide evidence to decisions made by governments and regulators. If you have ever heard the phrase "evidence-based rulemaking," it is all about RIA.

Think for a moment about when you or your government draft an AI regulation. It is very simple to put pen to paper to bring an actual regulatory idea to life.

However, ideas and intentions do not always match reality, and as simple as this exercise is, you are not always aware of the consequences of the decision you are making.

Acting like this may have repercussions for businesses, investors, consumers, the environment and even for the government, the player who has to monitor and ensure compliance.

While you hope for the best when drafting and approving an AI regulation, wouldn't it be helpful to have some previous or ex ante evidence, data or indicators about its likely impact?

This is where AI RIA shows up to help you make better regulatory decisions.

AI RIA requires following a methodology. Countries implement RIA differently, but there is a common set of methodological steps regulators can take. Luckily, we have the OECD to tell us what a good RIA should entail.

One of their reports on regulatory impact analysis[15] outlines the following basic steps in the RIA process:

1. **Problem definition,** to describe the nature of the problem to be addressed, preferably in quantitative terms.
2. **Policy objectives and goals** of the regulatory proposal.
3. **Description** of the regulatory proposal.
4. **Identification of practical alternatives** to the regulatory proposal, as potential solutions to the policy problem in question.
5. **Analysis of benefits and costs** to compare the regulatory proposal and alternatives identified.
6. **Consultations and engagement** with potentially affected stakeholders and relevant experts.
7. **Identification of the preferred solution.**
8. **Defining a framework to monitor and evaluate the performance** of the selected option and anticipate the data required for that analysis.

Step 5, analyzing the benefits and costs of regulatory proposals and alternative solutions, is what many experts see as the central and most important part of RIA. It is where you get the evidence that will help you make a better decision. In theory.

In practice, I have seen what usually happens in many countries. Leaders invest a lot of resources and effort into getting Step 5 right. In most cases, the results are a total failure.

For AI RIA to succeed, you need to think differently. The methodological framework of the OECD remains very relevant. But your emphasis should shift to the earlier stages, starting with Step 1: Problem Definition.

I will keep saying it. *AI regulation should start with a problem. This is where you should focus your energy.*

When you know what the problem is, it will be way easier to find the right solution. This then takes you to Step 4, the other stage where you should spend enough time.

Once you know the problem, you should explore multiple ways to solve it. Of course, this includes the AI regulation you have in mind. But most importantly, you should consider other alternatives, some of which may not be regulatory or even the option of doing nothing and keeping the status quo.

The purpose of this exercise is not only to have alternatives and choose the best. Yes, that is part of it. But this step is also where you question whether your AI regulation is the best solution. This is where you start second-guessing yourself and playing devil's advocate.

"Wait a minute, are you saying I should question my awesome AI regulation idea? Don't you know that second-guessing makes me, my agency and leadership look weak?"

Yes, as ridiculous as it may sound, seasoned leaders like you or anyone aspiring to be one need to think out of the box and act differently to get different results. Better AI results.

The final chapter of this book will discuss this mindset shift in more detail. In the meantime, remember that your AI RIA should not die trying to be a PhD thesis that quantifies the costs and benefits of your AI regulation.

If you are going to die of something, it should be from understanding the problem that is hitting you from left, right and center. This includes finding alternatives to your initial idea to solve it. For this, you will need to talk and engage with others outside your government circle.

So, let's now move on and discuss public consultations.

Key messages to remember

- Every regulatory decision should originate from a real, context-specific public policy problem.
- An ex-ante regulatory impact analysis can be a great tool for improving AI regulations.
- Do not put all your energy into quantifying costs and benefits. Rather, focus on problem definition and on challenging your proposal by considering alternative solutions.

Procedural Fairness in Action

At the end of the last chapter, I discussed the concept of "psychology of procedural justice," also known as *"procedural fairness."* I said that it has to do with the process or how regulations are conceived and made.

In one of the quotes at the beginning of this chapter, I cited a paper by Lind and Arndt. They say that a fair process can take place in different instances within the regulatory process. As this chapter's quote says, one of these moments is during *"the hearings, meetings and online consultations used to design regulations."*[16]

We will return to the idea of fair process and how it is tightly linked to a consultation process. For now, let's go over why you need to take public consultations seriously, and how to conduct them effectively when drafting or reviewing your AI regulation.

Before we begin, I want to address the big elephant in the room in many conversations I have had with governments about consulting the public before approving regulations.

If you were an outsider listening to those conversations, at face value, your takeout might be that governments have a strong commitment to public consultation and participation.

Of course, I have yet to meet a senior government official who publicly opposes listening to citizens or the private sector.

But very few leaders put their money where their mouth is. When the rubber hits the road, and conversations get serious about how to run an open and transparent public consultation process, you can start feeling uneasiness in the air.

A former government counterpart once confided that colleagues at the center of power considered public consultations as *"too much transparency"* in decision-making.

Here we are. I am sure that if you are the type of person, leader or government official who agrees with the statement above, you are highly unlikely to be reading these lines.

I can also say that you are, or want to be, a different kind of government leader. A leader looking to do right and transform things for good.

So, let's discuss why and how to run proper public consultations on proposed AI regulation.

AI regulation is inherently complex. For starters, it is a new topic with many unknowns, especially for regulators. It is also a field that can get very technical. Just think about issues of cybersecurity or AI algorithm fairness, explainability or interpretability of decisions made by black boxes.

In this context, it is very tempting and natural to leave the design of AI regulation to experts who really understand the complexity and intricacies of AI.

However, a regulation that is technically sound content-wise can be a complete failure when implemented.

Why? Because, as Lind and Arndt tell us,

"The best-designed regulation is a poor tool for governing if it can only be enforced through constant surveillance and draconian punishment."[17]

Solutions or rules handed on a "silver plate," as appealing as they may be, will not only lack ownership but will also face compliance issues. This is because those affected by them may not understand or share their rationale.

For a solution to be effective, those affected by it need to be part of its creation process. This is one of the reasons public consultations are extremely important when planning AI regulation.

Thus, you have to open up and listen to broader audiences. This does not mean that experts should be excluded. It just means that they should not be your only source of feedback.

So, what is your next step?

Regardless of the channel(s) you use to conduct your public consultations, there are three basic actions you need to take, no matter what.

If you make an effort to get them right, your chances of achieving better AI results will increase significantly. Here is what you need to do[18]:

1. Give advance notice to the public and provide access to the text of your AI regulatory proposals before they are approved.
2. Create spaces where citizens, businesses and all affected or interested stakeholders can share comments and views on your AI regulatory proposals in a transparent, interactive and respectful way.
3. Publicly explain how participation was or was not used to modify and improve the content of your AI regulatory proposals.

Transparency, inclusiveness, two-way dialogue, respect and explanations are part of this type of consultation. All these characteristics contribute to a fair decision-making process.

They are also a great way to counterbalance the influence of big players in the AI industry, seeking to make rules favorable to their interests.

Once you are ready to do this and actually do it, you need to realize that consultations are not a one-off exercise. They are not something you do for box-ticking purposes or to "justify" your regulatory decisions and the move on.

Public consultation should function as an ongoing dialogue. It is not limited to the moment when you have the legal text of your proposed AI regulation. The real commitment is to engage stakeholders throughout the entire lifecycle of your regulation—not only when you want to approve a regulatory change.

For instance, while doing your AI RIA, you can get inputs on your problem definition or the identification of alternative solutions. You can also do so when publishing your AI regulatory plans, and especially to identify and understand implementation problems from existing regulations.

Below is a graphic representation of how public consultation should occur at every stage of the regulatory process.

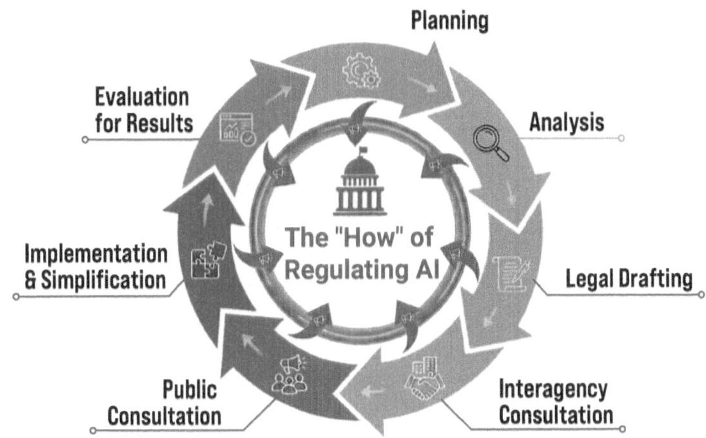

I am sure you can get creative with the details to make these consultations happen and feel real. To avoid falling into consultation fatigue, remember that there is a lot of power in listening.

You will need to become an expert in the skills that differentiate leaders from bosses: knowing how and when to listen to others.

To close this section, let's return to Lind and Arndt and the idea of procedural justice in psychology.

In their literature and quote at the beginning of the chapter, they say that the relevance of a fair process during proper consultation when designing rules can *"enhance acceptance of the rule-making process and of the regulations ultimately put forth."*[19]

When people perceive that rules are designed in a fair process, they are more likely to accept and comply with them, even if they might not agree with them.

Compliance with AI regulation is fueled by open, participatory, transparent and respectful public consultations.

However, the spillovers do not end with more compliance.

A robust consultation process on AI regulation increases the legitimacy of your rules and builds back trust in government.

By government, I mean your government and organization. The only one that matters to you.

If you want to learn more, including some empirical evidence on these effects, I recommend the work of Malesky and Taussig in Southeast Asia.[20]

<h2 style="text-align:center">Key messages to remember</h2>

- Public consultations are key to getting AI regulation right.
- A proper consultation process requires at least three basic actions: advance notice and access to your AI regulatory proposal; an open, respectful and two-way dialogue with the public; and explanations on how participation was or was not considered in improving the final AI rule.
- Consultation is not a one-off or box-ticking exercise. It should occur throughout the lifecycle of an AI rule.
- Beyond creating better AI regulations, with proper consultations you win on future compliance and build trust in your government and organization.

Publish What You Enact

During my early years at the World Bank, I worked with Dani Kaufmann, a governance and anti-corruption guru. He is not only smart but outspoken.

During our work together, I learned about the Publish What You Pay (PWYP) initiative, an international NGO advocating for financial transparency in extractive industries.

At that time, PWYP asked companies to declare how much they paid governments for the rights to extract oil, gas, minerals and other natural resources. This goal was to increase transparency and accountability, as well as reduce discretion in a sector where big money and big corruption are common.

What does this have to do with AI regulation?

It has to do with the principle of disclosing and giving public access to all AI passed laws and regulations—what we might *call Publish What You Enact.*

I understand if you have a big question mark in your mind. Publishing laws and regulations may sound like a natural thing for governments to do.

But believe me, I have witnessed how things are, especially in less-developed economies. There, maybe including your country, it is not always easy to find and get access to information about all existing regulations.

Countries have their Official Gazettes, but in many cases, those sources only deal with primary laws. Even within this subgroup of rules, in several countries, finding legal information online is not what you would call a user-friendly experience. Of course, there are a few good exceptions.

Things get worse when you are interested in secondary legislation. If it is a rule, like a decree issued by the president or prime minister, you may have more luck. They come from the head of state.

However, when you are looking for regulations approved by ministers and other regulatory agencies, things can get complicated and ugly.

If you start digging and browsing the websites of specific ministries and regulators, you will probably find a section with the laws and regulations under their mandate, including those they have created and implemented.

Again, the process is not user-friendly, as you have to visit multiple government websites.

Why is it so important to have easy public access to all laws and regulations? To all AI laws and regulations, specifically.

It all comes down to predictability and transparency.

Poor access to AI regulatory information may not be a case of big money and big corruption, like in the extractive industries, the focus of PWYP. However, it creates an unpredictable regulatory environment and opportunities for corruption.

Unpredictability comes from not knowing the obligations and constraints for firms operating in the AI space.

Opportunities for corruption come from the discretion government officials exercise when they talk about "some AI regulations" that nobody knows or has heard of, but are under their domain.

A simple solution to these problems is to build a single portal with all AI laws and regulations.

Actually, this should be done for all laws and regulations in your country. But at a minimum, do it for AI regulation.

Once you have your single portal, make it easy and user-friendly to search for information. You can even leverage AI for this—I will touch briefly on this suggestion in the final chapter of Part 2.

Key messages to remember

- Access to AI regulations should be simple.
- A consolidated portal with this—and ideally all regulations in your country—is a great starting point. It reinforces predictability and transparency.
- Once you have that, there are so many more things you will be able to do—including with the help of AI.

Simplify, Then Go Digital

Regulation has a snowball effect. You have likely seen it. As a seasoned leader, you probably know it. Regulation, along with the obligations and requirements that come with it, adds up almost exponentially.

The same happens with the administrative procedures that come to life when governments implement regulations.

Right now, your government is probably only dealing with a few national laws or, in some cases, just a national AI law.

Soon, secondary regulations and implementation mechanisms will follow. Then, licenses, product or activity registrations, algorithm registries and other information obligations on AI firms will join the party.

This is okay; it is part of the regulatory process. However, *you need to be aware that the more you request from firms, the more costs it creates for everyone.*

It is easy to understand that red tape imposes costs on AI firms. It is less obvious that this also creates costs for your government, as you need to monitor and enforce compliance with all the things you are asking from AI firms.

However, you are in a good spot. Although many existing laws and regulations already affect AI, most of the rules will be new. So, you are almost starting with a relatively clean slate. This presents an opportunity to get regulation right from the beginning.

What we have discussed so far in this chapter should help you come up with better and simpler rules.

This is your chance to act differently and achieve different results.

Hopefully, when you get to the implementation of AI rules, you have already embraced what PEMUDAH in Malaysia advocates for: *no more regulation than necessary.*

This should cascade to no more administrative requirements, licensing procedures, compliance steps, information obligations or similar red-tape demands than necessary.

If you are already in this place, then you are good to go digital. A simplified and streamlined regulatory procedure is at the sweet spot of readiness to become digital and simplify things even more.

But this ideal reality is extremely elusive. It is likely that your AI regulatory procedure will be born complex and burdensome.

A compound effect will happen when your AI regulatory procedures are combined with other procedures from existing rules that are not completely related to AI but affect it.

Here is my piece of advice: resist! Resist the temptation to go straight to digitalize AI administrative procedures.

It is becoming common and accepted knowledge that an offline mess will most certainly become an online mess. Unnecessary regulatory procedures do not magically disappear when they become digital.

So, simplify your offline AI-related procedures, requirements and services; then and only then, go digital.

While you go digital, do not forget to place emphasis on the UX/UI design of your AI-related digital services.

This is to ensure that the user experience, for instance, when registering an AI product with the government or requesting an AI license, is simple and straightforward.

I have visited many government portals where even making an appointment to receive a service is complicated, despite it being an online process.

Again, why not be creative and leverage AI to make your administrative procedures and services easier for AI firms, and of course, for you as a government leader?

- Administrative procedures are important to implement regulations, but they also tend to create unnecessary burdens on firms, the public and your government.
- Most governments focus on making these services digital.
- Before going digital, you must simplify them first. Otherwise, your offline mess will perpetuate online.

Don't Regulate and Drop the Ball

In my early years as a regulatory policy specialist, I started asking myself a fair question about something I had subtly observed. My colleagues, international organizations and experts placed great emphasis on governments adopting ex ante RIA (regulatory impact analysis).

Undoubtedly, it is great to "clean" or improve the quality of the flow of new regulations with the help of RIA. But I started wondering why there was no such emphasis on addressing issues with existing regulations— especially if there are a lot more of those issues with those rules affecting businesses and citizens now, in the present moment.

During a business trip, Lorenzo Allio—friend and international expert on better regulation— told me that it was easier to deal with the flow, which accounted for only a few rules, compared to the "sea" of thousands of existing regulations.

Later, talking to Bryan O'Byrne—international trade and regulatory specialist—, it became clear that an emphasis on ex ante RIA makes complete sense for countries that already have a good regulatory environment, like most OECD economies.

But let's get back to Lorenzo's point that dealing with new regulations is easier than addressing the humongous stock of existing government-made rules.

If you have had to review regulations as part of your government or leadership role, you know this: it is very difficult to review a large volume of them.

We are talking about millions of pages of legal text. It is not even simple to review a dozen regulations at a time.

With Jorge Velazquez and Ana Paola Gomez —international experts on better regulation—, we supported a few regulators in Colombia to pilot regulatory reviews, following a thorough and methodological approach.

As valuable, this type of review demands a lot of resources, both human and financial. You should also add the need for technical capacity within ministries, regulatory agencies and organizations reviewing regulation. The cherry on top would be the political willingness to embark on this technical process without, well, political interference.

The knee-jerk reaction to this reality goes like this: *"Okay, we have approved our regulation, that was a big win, so let's forget about it and simply move on."*

That is how governments usually forget about regulation for years, even decades. The status quo remains unchanged until political agendas shift or a crisis emerges, and the clock for quick changes starts to tick.

As a leader, what can you do about existing AI regulation?

Remember a key message from this book: *you have to actively manage regulation during its entire lifecycle.*

This implies not dropping the ball after you approve your AI rules. Instead, you should manage your regulation through implementation, identify ways to simplify it, improve compliance and finally review it after a few years to know whether it achieved its purpose or requires changes.

It sounds like a lot, right? I am not going to lie to you. It is a lot! This is why reviewing regulation is the "Achilles' heel" of regulatory policy.

However, things that matter are not always easy. That is why they matter. In addition, remember that you are almost starting from scratch. AI regulation will be only a sample of the entire regulatory universe in your country.

Sample or not, there are a few things you can do to be on top of your AI regulation, even after it has been approved. Let me rephrase this: especially after it has been approved. Here, I give you three recommendations.

The first piece of advice is what some countries call "sunset clauses." In a nutshell, this regulatory tool is used to force the review of regulations after a certain number of years of implementation. The timeframe could go from three to five years after enactment.

In its most rigid version, a sunset clause implies that the regulation ceases to have effect unless the regulator reviews it before its sunset date. This creates pressure for governments to review rules they want to remain valid.

But governments do not like this type of pressure. Why would they shoot themselves in the foot, right? That is why, in some cases, sunset clauses just trigger a regulatory review without ending the life of the rule in question.

Regardless of its setup, a sunset clause for AI regulation is a great fit. Why? Because AI is new and constantly evolving.

Even if you get AI regulation right today, the sure-to-change context will be very different in a few years, with new innovations, uses, issues and unknowns.

For this reason, sunset clauses give AI regulators an opportunity to adapt, not drop the ball for decades, and make sure that their AI regulation remains relevant, without trying to catch up from a thousand miles behind.

My second piece of advice concerns the constant consultation role you should have during every stage of the life of a regulation.

More than doing formal consultations, I am talking about a dialogue, which could be informal in some cases.

The premise behind this idea is that innovations like AI do not emerge spontaneously. Yes, I have said that AI is new, but that is in comparison to other things.

Innovations can be disruptive, but they take time to evolve and become what we see when they go mainstream.

This presents an opportunity for regulatory agencies to be part of this process. To seize this opportunity, you have to be proactive, not dormant, and a good listener. Otherwise, you will be left behind while the markets and industries you regulate change.

A close dialogue between you and AI firms is not only important; it should be part of your performance evaluation. It sounds simple, but it requires a change of culture, and a change of mindset—we will talk about this in the book's final chapter.

However, there is more than having dialogue with the AI industry. To keep up with or plan for evolving changes in AI, you have to do something at some point.

If innovations are still emerging and not ready for new regulation, you can consider regulatory sandboxes. This tool creates a space for firms to test innovations like AI in a controlled environment, while regulators learn about it. I will elaborate on sandboxes in the next chapter.

My final recommendation builds on what I have mentioned a couple of times in this chapter. Get creative and use AI to help you review existing and new regulations.

Chapter 7 will tell you a little more about that. I am happy to help you and your government with both: the "how" to regulate AI and how to use AI to regulate better.

5

Regulation That Enables AI's Growth

"When done well, regulation is as much of a core driver of innovation for emerging markets as is the technology or humans behind it."

—Jaime Leverton

"Regulation should not be seen as a burden but as an indispensable enabler of innovation."

—Stan Zurkiewicz

Having gone through the "how" of regulating AI, we are now at the point where we need to start talking about the "what" of regulating AI.

As I said in the introduction, I will not get into the details of specific AI regulation that needs to be created.

This means that without knowing the specific context and issues AI is creating—or not creating—in your country, it becomes a pointless exercise to claim that a specific topic should be regulated.

This is the same mistake governments and non-state actors make when calling for regulation based on perceptions, fears or even good intentions.

In the last chapter, you learned how to identify and understand problems before drafting AI regulation. But this does not mean you should wait passively for problems to arrive before identifying them.

As a leader, you know that better results are more likely to happen when strategic minds foresee how things may evolve before they actually happen. This is a trait of visionary leaders, sometimes natural, sometimes developed.

My intention in this chapter is to nurture that vision by highlighting strategic areas where regulatory decisions can make the difference between success and being left behind in the AI race.

Let's start with regulatory reforms and tools that will enable AI's growth. Inspired by Professor Hiroki Habuka's[2] classification of Japan's AI regulations,[21] I will call this group: *Regulation for AI.*

Regulation to Build Your Digital Infrastructure

*T*here are many elements that make AI and GenAI possible. But some building blocks are more crucial than others.

---

2   Research Professor at Kyoto University and expert on AI governance.

For starters, there is no AI without data. That's that. No other way to go around.

All AI and GenAI tools and models you have used or heard of cannot exist or work without data. In the next chapter, I will discuss how this has created far-from-ideal market dynamics, resembling a new fever rush to get data—the new gold—in any possible way. Many times, unethically.

Before that, I want to tell you about a *crucial stepping-stone for AI models, firms and the entire industry to flourish: the digital infrastructure that powers AI.*

The general public may not be aware of this, but those in the AI industry certainly are. Even governments taking the AI race seriously, or at least making a real effort to jump on the AI bandwagon, already know it.

You cannot scale AI and reach its full benefits without the necessary digital infrastructure.

When leaders talk about this but do not act on it, they may just be repeating what other leaders said. Or they may not yet have internalized that digital infrastructure is an extremely important piece of the AI puzzle.

Before I touch on the role regulation has in this, let's dig into some of the core elements of AI's digital infrastructure.

Start with computer power. Every time you use an AI/GenAI model (ChatGPT, Gemini, Claude, Copilot or others) that creates images, text and more, you see them "thinking" or "working" before they deliver what you asked for.

For that "magic" to happen, AI models consume a lot of computer power. Let me repeat. *A LOT of computer power.*

A 2025 MIT article reports that generating an image with GenAI, which takes seconds, can use the same amount of energy as fully charging a smartphone.[22]

Put simply, computer power comes from GPUs, CPUs, microchips and other server components hosted in data centers that support cloud computing solutions.

GPUs, CPUs and microchips are made of different materials. Some are very common, like silicon and aluminum, while others include rare earth elements.

To build data centers, you need land. To power them, you need a lot of electricity. Because GPU servers and their components generate heat while storing data and performing their miraculous tasks, they require cooling, which adds more electricity and water demands.

In addition, reliable, high-quality internet services and an interconnected network of data centers allow AI models to store, retrieve and process data with low latency—or in less fancy words, at the fastest possible response time.

Of course, many more things need to happen for you to sit behind your screen and enjoy the benefits of AI's magic. But digital infrastructure is a key part of it.

As a user, you may probably never see all these foundations, and honestly, you do not need to. But as a leader, you must be aware of them when making decisions about AI.

Now, let's discuss how regulation applies to AI's digital infrastructure. I will focus on three key enablers: *investment, trade and competition.*

Building AI's digital infrastructure requires private investment, local and foreign. If you want to move fast, you will also need to help investors access land; access reliable services like electricity, water and internet; and finally, enable the import of hardware and other goods without too much of a hassle.

It is completely fair if, at this point, the connection between regulation and this entire agenda is still not entirely clear. Do not worry. It never is at first. So, let's make those links less blurry.

Let's start with investment. If your country is not a global economic power, you will be competing with other countries to attract foreign direct investment (FDI).

FDI and local investment can help your country build data centers, maybe manufacture microchips and other components, or simply boost your country's capacity to generate electricity and provide better internet services.

Yes, you can provide fiscal incentives and good deals to access electricity, water, land and other resources. But. There is always a "but." When your neighboring countries or competitors do the same or better, what do you have left to attract FDI or promote the necessary investment for your digital infrastructure?

At some point, improving regulation becomes all you have left to do, but instead of a last resort, see it more as your ace up your sleeve.

Remember what I said in the previous chapter, when I cited the World Bank's Global Investment Competitiveness Report?

The Top 3 factors considered by foreign investors when deciding which country to invest in are: political stability, macroeconomic stability and, you got it, a country's legal and regulatory environment.[23]

All three factors above are considered more important than fiscal incentives, market size or labor cost.

I will not get into the details of what you need to fix or reform to attract or promote investment for your AI infrastructure. Instead, I will just ask you a few questions.

How easy is the "investor journey" in your country? Is it simple for the private sector to formalize an investment idea or promise, like a new data center or an electricity plant? Or do they face a "nightmare" when starting a business in your country?

Less burdensome, simpler regulation, administrative and licensing procedures play a key role in attracting and promoting AI-related investments.

Assuming you succeed in this important first step, congrats! You then need to look at the effects of regulation once AI investments start coming into your country.

You should ask whether regulations affecting firms building your AI digital infrastructure are an enabler or constraint for them to compete fairly, grow, make a profit and not be distracted from productive activities, to comply with unnecessary red tape and other regulatory burdens.

If your answer falls more on the side of unnecessary constraints, it is time to review and reform those existing rules affecting firms building AI digital infrastructure. Chapter 4 already covers "how" to do it. Chapter 7 will give you a glimpse of how AI can help you do regulatory reviews.

Now, let's move on and talk about trade. Or more precisely, international trade. To build your local AI infrastructure, your country will need lots of goods produced in other markets. Think about servers, microchips or technology to generate more electricity—ideally clean energy—and cooling systems. The list is long.

In 2025, tariffs resuscitated as a major constraint on trade. Before this major shift, non-tariff measures (NTMs) were considered the most significant barrier to the exchange of goods between countries. Among NTMs, you have technical barriers to trade (TBTs).

In less technical words, most TBTs are regulations that determine a product's characteristics and required quality, and how it is produced, packaged and labeled. TBTs are also rules that prohibit the production, import, marketing and use of certain products. Overall, they are rules (more government-made rules) that impact international trade.

Let me get granular for a second. Imagine that your country needs semiconductors or GPUs. Semiconductors are mainly produced in Taiwan, Japan, China and the US Most GPUs sold by American companies are manufactured in South Korea and Taiwan. Other components like motherboards, RAM, and SSDs come from Asian countries including Vietnam, Malaysia and Singapore.

As a leader promoting AI in your country, you need to assess whether you have existing technical barriers (regulations) that will prevent you from trading at a lower cost with these economies that supply key and scarce components everyone will try to get to build their AI digital infrastructure.

So, you either negotiate trade agreements with them, or make a couple of changes such as making regulatory reforms that reduce existing technical barriers to trade, and simplifying and cutting red tape at your customs to facilitate the flow of these foreign-made goods into your country.

Finally, let's talk briefly about competition. Healthy and fair competition in markets is always good. It improves the quality of services, brings prices into balance, and kicks out firms that are unproductive or deliver poor services.

Regulation plays a key role in incentivizing healthy and fair competition, which is necessary for AI markets to flourish. This agenda goes beyond simply opening markets to new players.

Government-made rules can also help create good service standards and balance margins and prices in ways that allow better access to electricity, water or internet, thereby reducing the operating costs for AI firms.

Key messages to remember

- The digital infrastructure that powers AI is a crucial building block to scale AI in your country.
- Investment, trade and competition are three key factors influencing your capacity to build AI digital infrastructure.
- All three factors are highly affected by regulation. It is something not many leaders realize, but you should.

Create Space to Test AI Innovations

In addition to a digital backbone, technological innovation can benefit from an adequate playground. Not only to grow, but as the word *playground* implies, to play around, test and learn.

AI and previous waves of innovations have created products and services that do not exactly fit with their pre-existing reality. That is why they are innovations.

However, some of these innovations are disruptive. They completely break with the status quo, challenging it at its deepest center and taking everyone by surprise. Especially governments and their regulatory agencies.

Remember when I talked about the pacing problem? Disruptive technologies take this regulation—innovation dynamic to the extreme. Governments are not only forced to catch up, but they are prompted to react, and to do it quickly.

When Uber, Airbnb and other sharing-economy platforms entered the market, many people were fascinated by the new possibilities they brought for users and for those looking for a new job or source of income.

From a public policy perspective, the main discussions at that time revolved around fair competition, consumer protection, labor rights and, well, informality.

In many countries and cities, existing businesses and service providers, such as taxi drivers, established hotels, inns, or B&Bs were simply not happy with the new kids on the block. They were not licensed and did not comply with labor and other regulatory rules and costs applying to traditional businesses.

These established businesses and service providers, complying with existing rules, expressed their discontent through complaints, lobbying and other forms of pressure and influence. In some cities, they took justice into their own hands.

I still recall news from my home country, Mexico, where taxi drivers—part of unions or groups monopolizing services—simply did not allow Uber drivers to operate. How? Through direct confrontation and the use of violence.

If you have lived in or visited Cancun, you may have witnessed this situation. Local and foreign users attempting to ride an Uber are often harassed by organized taxi drivers.

Cancun's type of conflict and violence did not happen in every market where Uber, Airbnb and others started operating.

Aside from politics, the entrance of these new players created tensions and frictions that could have been handled better.

Regulatory sandboxes for AI are a solution your government can explore to create a better environment for innovative firms to enter the market, test ideas, and validate new business models before they scale up and go mainstream.

For this to happen, your regulators first need to acknowledge that disruptive AI business models are not always a threat and can bring significant value to consumers and markets.

The next mindset change is for regulators to shift from reacting and trying to catch up with AI innovation to actively engaging AI firms that deploy disruptive models. And why not decide to carve out a space for them to enter the market under circumstances that are both favorable to their innovations, and protective of the public good and other priorities regulators should care about.

More or less, this is the essence of regulatory sandboxes.

Without a formal definition, regulatory sandboxes are commonly understood as a controlled regulatory environment or "safe space," where firms can temporarily test innovation from new services, business models and products in real markets and with real consumers.[24]

The special thing about the sandbox is that firms entering it do not have to comply with all the existing regulations that typically apply to firms outside the sandbox.

Once inside, innovative firms work closely with and are supervised by relevant regulatory authorities.[25] Firms and regulators learn from activity in the sandbox at a lower risk level.

Regulatory sandboxes started in and have been used more extensively within the financial sector. They enabled the emergence and growth of many Fintech companies.

Sandboxes will be among the regulatory tools used to support AI. In fact, the EU AI Act—the most comprehensive existing AI legal framework worldwide, so far—requires all its member states to ensure that *their competent authorities establish at least one AI regulatory sandbox at the national level, which shall be operational by August 2, 2026.*"

So, what do you need to know, strategy-wise, about regulatory sandboxes?

In practice, regulatory sandboxes require a foundation to be effective. For starters, countries need to have a legal or regulatory framework to govern the creation and implementation of sandboxes. These are the rules of the game that delineate who can apply to be in the sandbox and under which conditions.[26]

Some countries have failed at this step because their sandbox framework ends up being too rigid to allow enough firms to enter and efficiently test their innovations.

Another key piece is the constant dialogue I mentioned, which needs to flow back and forth between regulators and AI firms. This is probably the most difficult part.

For it to happen, all parties must be willing to engage in a more flexible and non-traditional approach.

Regulators need to be more open to new ideas and models that do not match the legal frameworks they have created. Firms have to stop playing smart with government rules and their grey areas in their attempt to hit first and hard.

The last part may sound counterintuitive for firms, as there is always the possibility of a collective action problem when some players choose the free highway. Thus, governments need to be smart and create the right incentives that reward those taking the sandbox path.

There are many more lessons and pieces of advice on this topic. If you want to go deeper and zoom in on AI and regulatory sandboxes, a good place to start is a 2023 report by the OECD: "Regulatory Sandboxes in Artificial Intelligence."[27]

Key messages to remember

- Many of the unintended consequences arising from the emergence of disruptive technologies can be mitigated by creating the right space for innovation to grow.
- Regulatory sandboxes can create a space where firms and regulators learn from new business models and products in a controlled, more flexible regulatory environment.
- While conceptually appealing, the key is how you design and implement them.

Reforms to Remove Unnecessary Hurdles

In the previous two sections, we discussed regulatory changes and tools to create better conditions for AI innovations. Here, I want to get into regulatory issues directly affecting the creation and operation of AI firms.

Back in Chapter 2, I mentioned PEMUDAH, Malaysia's special task force to improve the country's business environment. As part of its values, PEMUDAH advocates for "no more regulation than necessary."

This is not a bad thing. Good regulations respond to actual problems and public policy objectives. The issues arise when rules do not originate from serving these goals or when they are ineffective and create obligations and requirements that are not necessary or aligned with those goals.

The result is: *more AI regulation than necessary.*

Balancing the right amount of regulation is more of an art than an exact science. As complex as this task is, you have to start somewhere. Otherwise, you might face a regulatory snowball effect.

A simple strategy is to focus your efforts on two larger groups of AI regulations:

1. the new AI regulations your government will be creating; and
2. the existing regulations already affecting AI firms.

The previous chapter should be your guide to dealing with *unnecessary hurdles from new AI regulations.* Here, I will recapitulate a few key messages.

When designing your new AI regulations, you know that you will face a lot of pressure. Internal pressure to come up quickly with the new AI rules. And external pressure to accommodate certain interests or, more generally, to avoid requirements that seem burdensome to an industry.

It is what it is, and there is little you can do to change this. But you can control the process or the "how" behind your AI regulation, and the questions you will ask during that journey.

You can control whether you really understand the problem you are dealing with before drafting your AI rules. You can control how you question your proposed solution and whether you explore alternatives that might better address the problem you are facing. You can control the type of dialogue you have with affected and interested stakeholders to gather more information and a clearer picture of your proposed AI regulation.

If you learn to get the most out of these things you can control, you will be better positioned to get closer to that balance of "no more AI regulation than necessary." Just remember that the "how" will be as important as the "what" you regulate.

Now, let's talk briefly about removing *unnecessary hurdles from existing regulations*. This is what many governments have in mind when they talk about a deregulatory agenda to eliminate regulations they say "stifle" innovation.

That is the agenda lately. Whether that philosophy is right or not, it is true that your government will have to deal with the legacy of existing regulations—including AI regulations created by your predecessors.

In the previous chapter, I talked about two ways to improve existing regulations. One was the digitalization of administrative and licensing procedures to facilitate compliance. The other was the frequent review of regulations to assess their continued relevance and business-friendliness.

Please review that chapter if you have to make those types of improvements. Here, I want to talk about two other regulatory approaches you could consider as strategies to give AI firms flexibility while reducing their compliance costs. I will discuss *outcome-based regulation and risk-based regulation*.

Governments tend to follow a "command-and-control" approach when drafting regulations. This means that their rules strictly dictate what needs to happen or not. Sometimes, the mandate is pretty vague, but still follows a logic of "you all have to do this, and in this way."

However, in many cases, the same regulatory requirements may not apply in all circumstances or even demand the same path for compliance.

For instance, if an AI regulation establishes obligations for personal data protection, it would be inefficient to require all AI firms to follow a single, uniform procedure or approach to make sure that the personal data they use is protected.

Similarly, it would be fairly reasonable to have a different set of regulatory requirements for a firm developing a chatbot than for a firm using AI-based facial recognition to identify potential criminals at airports. The stakes and consequences of failure in these two examples of AI systems are very different.

Outcome-based regulation, as its name suggests, focuses on creating rules that dictate the desired outcome rather than prescribing to firms the steps and details for achieving it.[28]

Let's take, for example, the potential gender, age, sexual orientation, race or political bias in LLMs (large language models) and AI applications.

An outcome-based AI regulation should focus on the principles or desired outcomes that ensure LLM and AI applications are unbiased. It should avoid being prescriptive about the details of how AI firms comply with that outcome.

AI regulations designed this way give AI firms more flexibility and the chance to explore different ways, including innovative approaches, to comply with AI regulatory requirements.

When AI firms have the liberty to innovate in how they achieve desired outcomes, they can also find and exploit competitive advantages through cost-efficient ways to align with AI laws and regulations.

For regulatory agencies, outcome-based regulation reduces the resources needed to monitor compliance with AI rules, as the focus is on outcomes rather than on a precise and prescriptive process to achieve them.

Because AI solutions will evolve quickly, this flexible approach also prevents the need to make constant changes to compliance requirements that become outdated as soon as new innovations appear around the corner.

Risk-based regulation is another approach that aims to reduce compliance burdens on both firms and regulators.

It functions under the premise that—within an economy, sector or industry—different activities present different risks, which require different degrees of monitoring and compliance techniques from regulatory agencies.

For governments, this implies that they do not have to monitor all firms the same way. Therefore, they can prioritize their efforts on firms that pose the highest risk.[29]

As an example, think about an AI algorithm responsible for self-driving or autonomous vehicles, and an AI algorithm that suggests to Netflix users the content they may like.

The level of risk of failure or problems in each AI tool is disproportionately different. Following a risk-based approach, your government should monitor more closely and impose more requirements on the use of AI in autonomous vehicles than on recommendations about streaming content.

When well designed and implemented, risk-based regulation reduces regulatory burdens for low-risk activities and targets regulators' efforts where they are most needed.

Key messages to remember

- As new AI regulations are created and begin to accumulate, it is very likely that your country will end up with more AI regulations than necessary.
- Review Chapter 4 on how to address this from the point of view of new AI rules and existing regulations affecting AI.
- Outcome-based and risk-based regulations are two more approaches you can consider to reduce burdens and create more flexibility for your governments and firms around monitoring and compliance.

A Better Business Environment for AI Firms

This final section is about something related to regulation, but that also goes beyond it. Here, I want to talk about a good business environment for AI firms to exist and grow.

It is highly likely that your country does not have a Silicon Valley or a Golden Triangle, like the US and the UK have. Maybe your government does not have the same resources as China, France, Germany, Canada and other countries to promote innovation in a complex industry like AI.

This does not mean that you should give up because the odds are against you. An underdog is still a dog.

A few weeks before I drafted these lines, I was in Ethiopia working with the World Bank. While in Addis Ababa, I joined the team for a field visit to the Ethiopian IT Park.

The still-developing IT hub is bringing together a mix of tech startups, data centers, research institutes and large companies.

The most rewarding part of the visit was talking to a tech firm that has been there since day one, when everything was just an idea, and the electricity supply was intermittent at best.

The conversation with the tech firm brought up the importance of regulation, including regulatory sandboxes. When we were introduced to the CEO of the IT Park, he raised many other necessary elements that contributed to making the hub a reality.

Whether Ethiopia will succeed with this IT Park or not is part of a different analysis. But examples like this raise more ideas about what countries can do when they lack a Silicon Valley, massive data center infrastructure like Virginia has or vast resources to promote AI as an industry.

Creating the conditions for an AI hub or cluster is an alternative that governments have to build a better business environment for AI firms and supporting industries to come together, support each other and grow.

It is a little like when leaders decide not to shine and get the spotlight, but instead create the necessary conditions for their team members to be the stars.

In the mix of enabling conditions, governments can contribute to helping AI firms and players shine in the country through infrastructure, financing, tax incentives and, of course, regulatory and policy changes.

For an AI hub, cluster or AI Park to evolve into something that delivers results in the future, it is not only about the government and the conditions it creates. It also takes the team that needs to shine.

The visit to the Ethiopian IT Park reminded me of some early research work I did during my first professional years at IPADE Business School in Mexico City.

At that time, I drafted a case study about the Triple Helix, a model for innovation based on the interactions and cooperation between universities, industry and governments.

One of the creators of the Triple Helix was a Dutch academic. Not surprisingly, the Netherlands has been implementing this approach to foster innovation in many industries. AI is not the exception, so I encourage you to learn about this model.

If you decide to explore a Triple Helix or similar initiatives to create a better business environment for AI firms, do not forget that regulation should be one of your cornerstones.

Actually, one of your first steps should be to identify all the regulatory changes needed to create better conditions and spaces for your AI industry.

As a government leader, you probably want your country to be recognized as the right place for AI innovation, vis-à-vis your neighboring countries and main competitors. When others start doing the same, your "secret sauce" or differentiator could be the better rules you create for AI's growth.

Key messages to remember

- Your country may not have all the chips other countries have to succeed in the AI game. But if you are at the table, you are still playing.
- In your case, it might take a village to develop your AI industry. Sometimes, your key contribution will be to create the right conditions for others to shine.
- Regulations are a very important ingredient of those "right conditions."
- Collaborative frameworks like the Triple Helix are just an example of how to promote innovation in your country.

6

Regulation That Protects Us from AI

"The safety of the people shall be the highest law."

—Cicero

"Artificial Intelligence will evolve to become a superintelligence. We need to be mindful of how it's developed and ensure that it aligns with humanity's best interests."

—Bill Gates

The last chapter was all about AI enthusiasm. About some of the strategic regulatory decisions that you should consider if you want to promote AI's growth in your country.

This chapter is more about the "blind side" of AI enthusiasm. The side you need to be aware of, even if you or those around you do not see or want to see it.

It is the side that needs to be protected. By protected, I mean protecting society from AI.

To enter this space, you need to be conscious that there is no good or bad AI. It is simply a tool. Yes, a powerful one, which people are getting to know and using more.

The good or bad connotation comes from how firms build AI solutions and how those firms and people then use them. The problems with AI originate in the human mind and actions behind it.

Let's bring this down to the world of regulation. In the last chapter, I shared a few strategic ideas about AI regulation, having in mind that AI can help humanity do good and bring positive change. Maybe, as some people say, AI will make it possible to cure cancer, save lives, improve education and much more.

As a leader, you need to see the other side of the moon and consider AI regulations to address undesirable behavior in its use.

My intention is neither to tell you about the specifics of this or that AI regulation, nor the particularities of their content. Everything starts with a context-specific problem or objective. So, my goal here is to add to your strategic thinking by raising awareness of issues that will require your attention sooner rather than later.

In this chapter, you will not hear about tools and solutions like in the previous one. The topics in this chapter are new territory.

However, when you get to the point at which you need to draft or amend AI regulations to tackle some of these issues, you will have the tools from Chapter 4 on the "how" to regulate. Those tools should be your guide at all times.

Let's get started with the conversation on "what" to regulate about AI. Concretely, to address the malpractices that are arising as AI use continues to expand. Professor Habuka calls this group *"Regulation on AI."*[30] Inspired by his classification, I will call them: *Regulation to protect us from AI.*

Key messages to remember

- AI enthusiasm might prevent you from seeing many issues that come up during the development and use of AI.
- As a leader, you need to be aware of these issues before deciding whether regulation or another approach is the best path to address them.

Data Privacy and Consent

I said it before. AI companies know it. The general public probably does not. As a government leader, you should be aware of this: *there is no AI without data.* Period.

As simple as this statement is, it has many consequences. The most important one is the craving and thirst for data that AI companies have. Why? Because data is the most essential input to train AI models.[31]

That is why AI firms would probably do anything to get the data they need for their models to work. The more data, the better. Some of them already have a lot. This universe also includes personal data. So, let's talk about it.

To be fair, collecting personal data did not originate with AI. Just think about all the personal data you provide online when you buy things, use social media or other online services.

This also happens offline. Like when you go to a physical store in the U.S., the cashier casually starts asking for your zip code, email and phone number.

In every single one of these occasions, we are, consciously or not, giving our personal data to firms and others. We do it with consent. Nobody is twisting our arms. We can say no and simply not get services from those businesses.

People may not like that others have and use their personal data. But, as Prof. Bruce Huang, my AI ethics professor at Harvard, said in class: *"If you want full data privacy, do not go online."*

Having said that, there are a few important issues related to data privacy and AI that you may eventually have to address with regulation.

One problem concerns what AI firms do once they have the personal data you gave them. The other issue has to do with a previous step in which you are not involved: the collection and use of your personal data without your consent.

A lot of what happens in the first scenario has to do with the fine print in the privacy policies and terms of use. That is the information we never read and instead decide to tick the box, giving our approval in some sort of autopilot mode.

The personal data AI firms collect includes the data you provide when opening an account or signing up for their services. There goes your name, email, date of birth, payment information, address and sometimes more.

While using their AI services, you are probably also sharing more personal data. In the case of GenAI, it is a combination of two things. You may be giving personal data when prompting the LLM, or the model may be looking for personal data publicly available on the internet—including yours—to answer your prompts.

I invite you to google *"Medium.com ChatGPT conversations could be used in court"* to realize that, as of today, your conversations are not private, and neither is the personal data you share in them.

That is the personal data many AI and tech platforms have. So, what happens next?

"Nobody knows" is probably a fair and honest answer. But let's explore what de jure means in the typical terms of use and policies that you accept.

A few AI platforms make clear that you own your data. They say that your personal data is yours and only yours. In some cases, they also give you the option to change settings, so your data is not shared or used.

When that happens, it is not the default option, and users are usually unaware of the chance to opt out.

Even when these statements are made, what remains very unclear are the specifics of how AI and tech firms use your personal data.

Many of them will say that they use your data to improve or perform the services they provide. They will also say that they may disclose your personal data to third parties, as part of their business activities, to serve you. They do this and more than you expect because it is what you agreed to.

I invite you to read the terms and policies of the AI platforms you use. It is a great exercise to understand how they use our personal data and other information we voluntarily share.

In the meantime, I will give an example from a conversation with a friend who was moving back to Mexico. In his new job, colleagues recommended using Taxdown, an AI solution that helps users know whether they have a positive balance with the tax authority and, if so, file a tax return.

My friend signed up for this service and was surprised when the AI platform showed information about a medical appointment he had. The data collected went beyond the costs and taxes of the medical bill, and included his medical provider and the services he received.

When he told me that, my initial reaction was that it was a clear abuse and a case of unnecessary data collection. But when I checked their privacy policy, it became clear that they collect that type of data and others, to—you guessed it—provide and improve their services, among many other things.

Like it or not, whether you are aware of it or not, this practice is something Taxdown's users agree to when requesting services.

This example gives you only a glimpse of what happens in practice with the data people share with AI firms. As a government leader, you should consider how to approach this issue, including possible regulatory responses.

The European Union has been a pioneer in this field with its General Data Protection Regulation (GDPR). More countries, probably yours, have passed or are approving data protection laws. They can serve as inspiration and reference.

However, do not forget that, as these legal mandates start to trickle down into secondary regulation, your rules need to respond to problems and public policy objectives that are specific to your country. Copying what the EU and others have drafted might not save the day.

My take on this first scenario is that your government can design obligations to make privacy policies and terms of use for AI service providers in your country more accessible.

The common practice of showing links to this information and a box users need to tick to indicate agreement to those conditions, which nobody reads or understands, might be effective in providing legal protection to AI firms, but not to consumers.

A more nuanced obligation, in which users have to tick several boxes for specific and important terms they are agreeing to, might be more effective at letting them understand how their personal data will be collected and used.

It is similar to what already happens in Europe when you visit a website, and decide whether to accept or deny cookies. You have to tick many specific boxes to allow the service to collect information about your online activity.

To close this section on data privacy and consent, let's talk briefly about the second scenario I mentioned: cases when *your personal data is collected and used without your consent.*

Imagine, for example, that you are walking down the street. It is a public space, just like the internet. Without you even noticing it, a camera or a set of cameras starts collecting data from you.

You may hesitate and ask: "What data?" Well, the camera could be tracking your movements, recording your voice and location, trying to determine your demographics and other characteristics, and even identifying you through facial recognition software.

You may not believe it or may decide not to think about it, because life is better when we do not pay attention to these things. Nonetheless, your data, our data, is being collected by cameras. Not only police surveillance cameras, but also cameras in retail stores, cameras from smart glasses, and yes, your doorbell camera and others inside your home.

Just like AI voice assistants are always listening, waiting for your questions or commands, which by the way has also raised data privacy concerns[32] when smart glasses became mainstream, we might reach a point where cameras are always "looking" and collecting data from you.

A prelude to this is a Forbes story that told the world how two Harvard students used Meta's Ray-Ban smart glasses and software they developed to access personal information from people on Harvard's campus.[33]

It remains unknown how much personal data these cameras collect, and for what purpose—maybe with the exception of police cameras. And it is not only cameras. This includes any technology that collects data without consent.

As a government leader, you need to be aware of these practices, understand the problems and risks they create, and then evaluate the best course of action to address them, including the potential need for regulation.

Key messages to remember

- The fact that there is no AI without data has created undesirable behavior by tech firms in how they collect and use data, including personal data.
- This includes both personal data collected with and without people's consent.
- Either through regulation or other means, there should be a better way for users to understand how the data they provide is used, and for firms to obtain consent instead of assuming that personal data is simply up for grabs.

Data Collection and Intellectual Property

Now you know that without data, there is no AI, and that this creates a frenzy in AI firms to collect as much data as possible. They need it to train and improve their models.

However, you also need to be aware that data collection by AI firms is not limited to personal data. It goes beyond that.

For a second, let's think about what kind of data you would need to train a GenAI model that creates any kind of image you ask for.

Simplifying things, you need to train the model with as many images as you can, so it learns about them, and can then create weird images like a unicorn, a dragon, your country's president, and Roger Federer playing a doubles match on a cloud barely above water full of pink sharks with elephant ears trying to eat them! Weird stuff, right?

Where is the best place to get all these images to train your model? Of course, you go online and scrape all the images you need, right? The internet is where this information is publicly available and free. Wait a minute, is it?

This is a great conversation to have with a friend or someone not related to these domains. The starting point is that if something is online, it means it is public. Fair point.

An interesting discussion comes when many of us think or thought that because something is publicly available, it means that we can use it for our needs.

If we agree or believe this is right, then it means that data on the internet is simply up for grabs for anyone to take and use. The quintessential data example of low-hanging fruit.

However, try to put yourself in the shoes of the creator of that content available online. This is a very diverse group.

You have authors, columnists, journalists, researchers, academicians, musicians, designers, photographers, artists and a long list of content creators. This list also includes cases when you post on social media, your blog or your business website that sells products and services.

If you are in this group, would you be okay with the idea that your data or content is up for grabs? Like your pictures on social media, or the article you published?

Yes, it is publicly available and technologically possible to collect it. But does that mean that it can be used by anyone without proper permission, recognition and remuneration to the creator of that content?

This is an issue of intellectual property that you need to address,
either by adopting a new or revised set of rules that better respond to
the current situation or through better enforcement of IP laws and
regulations.

You know what? Businesses and individuals creating content shared online are already taking matters into their own hands.

When you visit a website or online service, try reading its terms of service. In addition to clearly stating that they own the copyright to their content, many sites explicitly mention that they prohibit scraping.

Although sometimes unethical, scraping is still technically possible. That is why content creators look for tech to fight bots scraping their content. Despite many solutions, content continues to be used without authorization, and there are indications of black markets and illicit acquisition of proprietary data.

When resources are exhausted and there is some evidence of these malpractices, lawyers are called into action.

There are nowadays many lawsuits and class actions in which content creators have accused AI firms of copyright infringement for using data to train their models.

Big tech firms are among the defendants. Some well-known firms like Getty Images are among the plaintiffs. If you want to learn more, just search online for *"AI data lawsuits."*

To wrap up this section, I want to tell you that this and other issues will continue to emerge. You need to first be aware of them and understand what is happening before you decide to pull the trigger on new AI regulations.

For instance, in the months before I drafted these lines, news articles indicated that web traffic and clicks were significantly decreasing. Depending on the source, the drop rates range from 15–18% to 60–64%.

Why is this happening? Because of AI-powered search that now gives you AI Overviews of what you are googling.

In some cases, these overviews are so useful that you do not have to go from site to site to get the information you want.

But the big issue is precisely there. Without the content on those sites, the AI Overview would not be possible. Those sites being left out are the source of information. When some of these sites get lower traffic and fewer clicks, they also get less revenue. Food for thought.

Key messages to remember

- Data collection frenzy is not limited to personal data. To function, AI needs all types of data.
- A lot of proprietary data is being collected without proper permission, recognition and remuneration of content creators.
- This practice infringes on intellectual property and impacts the revenue of content creators, while AI firms reap the benefits.

Deepfakes, Identity Theft and Fraud

I am not sure if deepfakes started mainstreaming as a funny evolution of memes. I just remembered seeing, one day on social media, very realistic images of unthinkable celebrities and players wearing my soccer team's jersey.

Things got scary when it was not only images, but also videos showing a person's face in a body that was not theirs and in situations they had never been in.

I also recall that at some point, one guy made a video explaining how he was able to "recreate" Obama's voice with the help of AI.

As a citizen of the world and consumer of social media content, you probably have heard about some of the famous deepfake scandals: a fake explosion at the Pentagon that made waves in the stock market; President Trump being arrested; and the unfortunate explicit images of Taylor Swift. The list goes on and will continue to do so.

All these cases are about famous people and places, which seem to make their impact more salient. At the same time, as a government leader, you may be thinking about the potential consequences this could have in your country.

From a political angle, the deepfakes of Ukraine's President calling his troops to surrender, or former President Biden's fake "robocalls" asking Democrats not to vote in the New Hampshire primaries, can give you a glimpse of how fragile the stability in your country may be if deepfakes are used quickly to misinform the public.

However, deepfakes are also negatively affecting ordinary people, especially women. It is highly unfortunate that among this group are teen girls who are being victims of cyberbullying from school classmates, creating deepfake nudes of them.

In this last case, the problem is not only AI users creating the explicit deepfakes of teen girls, but also the "nudify" AI apps that are making this possible and easier to do.

Having grown up in Mexico, I can also see how deepfakes can be used by criminals doing financial scams, extortions and other types of cons and impersonation. And it is already happening.

Among the most vulnerable to these deceptions are the elderly and other groups with less digital skills. Even children and teenagers who are tech savvy but have less exposure to and awareness of the wrongdoings of other people are also at higher risk.

What should you do as a leader? I am with you if you think this problem goes beyond regulation and involves law enforcement, criminal investigation and similar areas.

While your legal and regulatory solutions should address your country's specific problems, some countries are taking steps and doing something about deepfakes.

In May 2025, the United States approved the "TAKE IT DOWN Act." It is a federal law to combat the distribution of nonconsensual and explicit images, either real or deepfakes. I like the name in all capital letters. It tells the public the severity and importance of this issue.

Among its measures to protect children and other victims of digital exploitation, this law requires platforms to remove this type of content upon notification. Still, it is not the perfect solution as the problem runs deeper, but it is a place to build on.

A few months after the U.S. Government passed the TAKE IT DOWN Act, Denmark also took a step forward on deepfakes.

The Danish Government announced a bill proposing to use its existing Copyright Law to grant citizens rights over their body, voice and facial features as a way to protect them from AI-generated deepfakes.

Whether these laws and others to come are effective enough is yet to be seen. They will also be facing an evolving AI landscape and, most likely, will have to be adapted and revised as malpractices change.

When you are ready to enter this space with a potential legal or regulatory solution, go back to Chapter 4 and remember that "how" you regulate this issue will be equally important to the final regulatory text your government approves.

In some of these cases, like the explicit deepfakes of women, teen girls and minors, one of the most important steps in the "how" to regulate is to put in practice what I have shared on procedural fairness.

Victims of deepfakes deserve to have a voice, be heard, be treated with respect and be part of the solution.

Decisions Made by "Black Boxes"

Good Intentions, Bad Outcomes. It is the title of a book by Santiago Levy, Mexico's former Deputy Minister of Finance and VP at the Inter-American Development Bank, until he retired.

His book has nothing to do with AI. Rather, it talks about how the Mexican Government followed all the textbook macroeconomic policy recommendations from Washington and still had poor economic growth results.

The title of his book has a parallel with what is happening with some AI models and solutions. They are created with good intentions, like helping schools or companies navigate thousands of applications to find the best candidates. Or maybe to help banks better determine whether to give a mortgage or vehicle loan to a client.

These are AI uses by the private sector. Let's think for a moment about possible AI-assisted decisions within your government.

For instance, AI that helps your government decide a citizen's eligibility and access to social and welfare programs. Or AI that makes recommendations to the police and judges, with a potentially significant impact on your freedom.

As we do this mental exercise, why not imagine AI assisting in decisions on who gets a vaccine first if we face another global pandemic like the 2020 one?

You can see that the stakes in all these situations could get really high. Even when people are not facing decisions made 100% by AI, but rather AI-assisted ones, they would want these decisions to be transparent, fair and well-explained.

Yet, that is not always happening. Thus, we are living the part of Santiago Levy's book title that comes after "Good Intentions." We are often getting "Bad Outcomes," or to put it more bluntly, unintended outcomes from decisions made with AI's help.

Even when AI-assisted or AI-made decisions end up being more effective from an economic, social, democratic or other perspective, *there will always be reluctance and distrust from the public and those affected if these decisions come from "black boxes" nobody understands.*

What can you do? Let me share briefly a little about Brazil and its AI bill, or *Projeto de Lei 2338/2023.*

The EU AI Act was the world's first comprehensive AI law. It is a great reference, just like Brazil's 2023 AI legislative proposals by Senator Rodrigo Pacheco.

The bill classifies AI by risk level, as the EU AI Act does. But what I found most interesting was Section II, which is all about rights.

In 8 articles and their respective paragraphs, Brazil's AI bill aims to give rights to people affected by AI.

For example, Article 5 talks about the right individuals have to receive explanations about decisions, recommendations or provisions made by AI systems, as well as the right to contest those decisions that have judicial consequences or that significantly impact the interests of the affected person.

These types of rights are a great starting point for your government to consider. I suggest you review Brazil's AI bill.

As you start this journey and define possible legal and regulatory solutions for your government to address decisions made by "AI black boxes," there are a few things you need to have in mind.

Among the factors falling under the umbrella of "algorithmic transparency," there are three you should consider: interpretability, explainability and AI fairness. Together, all three increase the trustworthiness of AI solutions.

Interpretability is all about making it possible for people to understand "how" an AI model functions. This is extremely relevant because algorithms and tools are becoming more sophisticated, and it is difficult for the public to understand the logic and inner workings behind their decision-making processes.

Explainability of AI (XAI), although sometimes interchangeably used with interpretability, focuses more on the "why" and justifications for AI decisions.

XAI is not about the inner workings and structure of AI models, but more about the reasons behind their outputs and decisions. DeepSeek and now Gemini are examples of models that include explainability elements as part of their prompt responses. However, not all GenAI models walk you through their reasoning process when you ask them something.

The general public is not necessarily interested in the inner workings and structure of an AI model, but most people would like to understand its reasoning when it makes decisions that affect them.

That is why XAI is very important for instilling public trust in AI solutions, and something you should be thinking about when planning AI regulations to deal with decisions made by AI models that resemble black boxes.

But—there is always a but—even in circumstances where AI models are very interpretable and explainable, there will always be cases in which people affected by AI decisions will simply consider those decisions unfair.

Rather than a fact, fairness is a perception. It is subjective. However, this does not mean there is nothing AI firms, or you as a government leader, can do about it.

AI fairness is usually thought of as preventing discrimination caused by biases in AI models, and we will talk about that soon. However, it is also about procedural fairness. Remember that we talked about it in Chapters 3 and 4? Let's briefly revisit this concept.

I said that in the field of regulation, procedural fairness or justice implies that when people perceive that rules are designed through a fair process, they are more likely to accept and comply with those rules, even if they do not agree with them. I said that to explain that the process leading to a regulation matters, too, not only the output or outcomes.

The original concept of procedural fairness was about decisions. Court decisions to be precise. So, if in the paragraph above, you substitute "rules" for "decisions," you will see that: *when people perceive that decisions are made following a fair process, they are more likely to accept those decisions, even if they do not agree with them.*

This can include decisions made by AI models. It sounds wonderful, right? The key is how AI firms, or you as a government regulator, put policy measures in place to make sure AI decisions follow a fair process.

You can read more about this topic in my publication "fAIr & square" at Medium.com. Here, I will quickly share four elements that are necessary for people affected by AI decisions to perceive they have been treated fairly. They are inspired by the literature on procedural justice or fairness, including work from Yale Law School, Berkeley Law and, of course, Lind and Arndt.[34]

- Having a voice in the matters or decisions that are affecting them;
- Being treated with respect and dignity by those making decisions;

- Receiving explanations about final decisions and outcomes; and
- Knowing that the decision-maker is transparent, neutral and has trust-worthy motives.

There are many ways to make these four key elements real. Just do not forget the importance of giving serious consideration to AI fairness. Besides creating trustworthiness around AI, it contributes to people's acceptance of decisions made by AI, even when those decisions are unfavorable to them.

Key messages to remember

- There is already reluctance about AI-made or AI-assisted decisions that come from "black boxes" nobody understands.
- Explainability is key to bringing transparency and clarity to the reasoning AI models follow.
- Trustworthiness in AI also comes from a fair process that combines voice, respect, explanations and good intentions around decisions supported by AI.

Biased Decisions and Models

Not all issues with AI decisions are related to black boxes. I kept this section separate because there has been significant controversy about bias in AI decisions.

Biases come from many sources: from the data used to train AI models and from the way algorithms are built. Basically, there is human bias among individuals involved in creating AI.

The big controversy comes from AI bias at the output and outcome level. A widely discussed example is Amazon's initial recruiting algorithm, which was not filtering female candidates because the data used in training the model reflected male attributes. However, concerns go beyond this type of result.

Among the main concerns about AI bias is the idea that AI will not only continue and perpetuate existing human biases, but will also amplify their effects.

If certain groups, either social, economic, racial, political, etc., have been historically favored or discriminated against, it is easy to understand the concerns that these situations will continue or worsen with a powerful technology that is already creating a lot of the content we consume and will be making more decisions that impact our lives.

A simple example to explore is the answer you could get if you ask a GenAI system to create an image of a successful executive and a stay-at-home parent. How high are the odds that the first image will be of a white man and the second of a woman? Probably pretty high. That has been the historical mental archetype or bias Western society has had.

This example may sound inconsequential—although it is not—because we are talking about an image. However, it reflects how AI solutions are often trained. It also gives us a glimpse of the consequences of more impactful decisions, like trying to identify criminals through facial recognition systems or other predictive policing algorithms.

In those higher-stakes situations, the thinking, theories and preconceptions behind AI models matter a lot, because they sometimes carry a lot of baggage.

So, what is for you as a leader to do about this?

It is great that data scientists are already discussing techniques to reduce individual and group biases in AI algorithms.

From a legislative perspective, it is important that any existing law protecting people from discrimination is applied to AI decision-making. The type of rights outlined in Brazil's bill is also highly relevant for protecting people from AI. The EU AI Act is another great reference.

For example, it is very likely that your government requires certain foods to be packaged, labeled or processed following certain requirements to protect consumer health. The same thing happens with brakes and many components of your car, so you can be safe even if you have an accident.

So, yes, at some point, AI laws will have to trickle down into AI regulations that are more specific about how to address issues like bias and other concerns we have discussed.

As you enter this space, remember that everything starts with a real and context-specific problem. Then, follow what you have learned about "how" to regulate.

Will this type of future requirement and standards on AI solutions hinder and stifle innovation? Most likely.

Despite the economic and political interests around AI, you need to understand that this and future innovations are meant to serve humanity, not the other way around.

In some cases, it is okay for regulations to stifle innovation. They are not created to serve only economic interests. Regulations are also there to protect desirable public goods.

That is why, in addition to creating regulations that enable AI's growth, you will need regulations that protect people in your country from AI. Let's talk about a couple more topics on this.

- AI's thinking is not something "pure." Like most things created by humans, it comes with biases from those who designed and developed it.
- At some point, your government will have to find solutions to perpetuated social, economic, racial and other types of bias in AI solutions.
- As you face opposition from AI firms about new requirements and obligations that "stifle" innovation, remember that rules are there also to protect the public, not just to serve innovation.

The Environment

In the previous chapter, I mentioned that AI requires computer power to operate. Much of that computer power comes from GPUs, CPUs and other microchips, components of servers located in data centers.

This is why countries competing to be at the forefront of the AI race are significantly investing in, or creating better conditions and incentives for, huge private-sector investments in data centers and the digital infrastructure that AI demands.

I already talked about the regulation to make this happen. Now, it is time to talk about the price the world needs to pay to have an AI party. This is the part that not many AI enthusiasts want to see or talk about, and the part you need to be aware of.

It is the impact AI's digital infrastructure will have on the environment and natural resources.

When people, including myself, say that AI requires a lot of computer power, you need to think beyond data centers with more servers and more powerful chips and processors to store and analyze data. *You need to recognize that the impressive artificial thinking happening there is powered by electricity.*

It is fair to say that many things nowadays require electricity to function. So, how much electricity are we talking about when discussing AI's needs?

A 2025 report from the International Energy Agency (IEA)[35] gives us a good picture of how AI's use is driving the electricity demand from data centers.

The IEA estimates that electricity needs from data centers worldwide will double by 2030, accounting for more than Japan's current total electricity consumption. Yes, Japan! A high-tech and industrialized country.

Similarly, in the U.S., a 2024 report from the Department of Energy[36] found that data centers consumed 4.4% of total U.S. electricity in 2023. By 2028, the DOE expects this figure to be between 6.7% and 12.0%.

As impressive as these numbers are, sometimes we need examples from our daily lives.

The MIT article[37] I mentioned before, which states that creating an image with GenAI consumes the same energy as fully charging a smartphone, also reports that using a dollar's worth of GPU, or computer power time, emits a similar carbon footprint to driving 5–20 miles in a gas-powered vehicle.

Things do not stop here. Just as people say "my head is burning" when thinking hard, GPUs, CPUs and other micro components physically overheat from working hard to meet AI's demands. These parts and the temperature in data centers require cooling.

Cooling down AI's "brains" requires more electricity—we already talked about that—and water, used for air conditioning and immersion or direct-to-chip cooling techniques.

Just like we discussed electricity needs, it is important to know how much water we are talking about.

For starters, the Lawfare Institute reports[38] that a small data center (with a capacity between 1 and 5 megawatts) consumes 26 million liters of water per year—similar to the yearly average water consumption of 62 families in the U.S.

To put things in perspective, the Lawfare Institute also explains that by the end of 2024, total U.S. data center capacity was over 40,000 megawatts. Based on this figure, they estimate that water demand from data centers equals the average annual water consumption of more than 2 million families.

Similarly, an NPR article mentions[39] that a medium-sized data center uses 300,000 gallons of water per day, about the amount used by 1,000 U.S. households. Furthermore, the University of Illinois reports[40] that a large data center consumes, per day, water equivalent to that used by 4,200 people.

As AI use continues to expand, it will demand even more electricity and water. If the increasing demand for energy is not matched by an increasing supply of cleaner energy, the environmental impact of AI could be considerable.

In the state of Virginia, a data center powerhouse in the U.S., with large percentage of the world's traffic passing through it, there have been concerns that rising energy demand from data centers will prevent the state from transitioning to clean energy and will increase its reliance on methane gas.[41]

Water, being a scarce and vital resource, will also be a topic of huge debate as its use in data centers begins to constrain its availability for human consumption, farming and other vital activities.

The American Society of Civil Engineers reported[42] that in Oregon, there was a legal battle because data centers' water consumption in the region tripled between 2016 and 2021. In Dalles, this accounted for more than 25% of the town's annual water consumption.

This is just a glimpse of the pressure AI's growth will put on the environment and natural resources. You can add potential issues related to rare earth minerals and distortions in electricity prices for consumers and other businesses.

As a government leader, you will probably face a regulatory race to the bottom, in which incentives from global competition might skew your decisions towards lax rules that will not properly protect the environment, natural resources and consumers.

But here we are, 100-plus pages into this book. If you are still reading, my guess is that you are or want to be a different type of leader. A leader who wants to do things right.

My advice continues to be that "how" you regulate AI matters equally or even more than "what" you regulate. So, if needed, go back to Chapter 4, where I discussed this "how."

The section titled *"Identify the Problem and Question Regulation as the Best Solution"* is all about RIA, or ex-ante Regulatory Impact Analysis.

RIA helps you assess and understand the potential consequences of new regulations before you approve them.

Among the several consequences you can explore through RIA are, you got it, the impact of AI regulation on the environment, natural resources and consumers.

The tool is there for you to learn and use. I did not call that section of the book "Regulatory Impact Analysis" because I wanted to emphasize the part of the RIA methodology that requires you to first understand the problem you are facing, explore alternatives to your AI regulation idea, and question whether it is the best solution.

I am not going to lie to you, doing RIA requires more time and effort than simply getting your pen, putting your ideas and best intentions on paper, and then passing your AI regulations.

This is a step not many government leaders take. They see it as a hassle. As something limiting their capacity to regulate on a fast track. I see it as a wise and responsible thing to do.

Key messages to remember

- AI requires a lot of computer power to function, which significantly increases demand for electricity and water to keep data centers functioning.
- This is already having an impact and will continue to grow as AI use scales worldwide.
- As a leader, you need to be aware of and understand the impact AI's growth and your AI policies will have on the environment and natural resources.

Your Job, Your Kid's Job

So far, I have presented you with some issues about AI I believe you need to be aware of. There are, and there will be many more. When you decide to address them with AI regulation, go back to Chapter 4 to refresh your ideas about the "how" you should approach those regulatory decisions.

However, there is one last topic I want to tell you about. This is an issue that has been part of some science-fiction movies, books and tales. It is an issue that people are already talking about and that is slowly showing its face to the world.

It's the issue of AI taking over your job. Or, what could be even scarier for a parent, AI taking over your kid's job.

Before I tell you about the issues that are already emerging, let's go over some of the AI enthusiasm that is preventing this topic from being discussed more broadly.

Innovation and disruptive technologies always bring change, and change, like it or not, brings opportunities to some and uncertainty to others.

When it comes to AI and people's jobs, the typical message goes like: "AI will increase productivity by helping people with burdensome tasks that demand time and attention nobody has nowadays," or "People will finally have time to focus on things that matter."

To a greater extent, those statements are true. If you are using AI, you know it. However, a good question to ask is whether this is the only outcome that will really happen.

Think about designers, for example. How is the demand for their services being affected?

With AI, you can now create logos, covers, and many other design outputs. Or you can work with a less experienced designer who uses AI, and still get pretty good results. All of this, at a significantly lower cost and in less time.

Web designers, authors, customer service providers, travel advisors and many other professions are gradually experiencing competition from AI solutions. Some of them are using it to stay updated and in the game.

These dynamics are expected to accelerate quickly.

The speed with which human beings could be left out of the labor market equation due to AI should not be overlooked.

Economists tell the world about the Schumpeterian "creative destruction" dynamic, in which AI will replace old jobs while creating new jobs.

The World Economic Forum, in its *Future of Jobs Report of 2025*,[43] already gave some indication of this. It says that AI is expected to create 11 million new jobs by 2030, but in the same period will displace 9 million jobs—more than any other technology.

The argument that with AI, some jobs will disappear while others will be created is true, but it is usually advocated more by those who benefit the most from AI or similar innovations.

In a market economy, this group is represented by people who own more capital or are capable and talented enough to innovate and create value.

But what does that mean for the majority of people? Are they going to have to wait for market dynamics to settle? What kind of jobs will be created? Better jobs?

I have written about this in my Medium publication called "fAIr and square." There you will find more on this and other topics covered in this book.

In the meantime, I want to go back to the point where I promised to tell you about what is already happening. About the impact of AI on jobs that traditionally were meant for your kids and other young professionals.

A study by Oxford Economics[44] and media reports indicate that recent college graduates are facing difficulties finding employment because entry-level positions are being displaced by AI.

Many of us had entry-level jobs that required less experience. They served an important purpose in an early transition from school to work and in developing professional skills.

As those positions demand less strategic thinking and are highly prone to automation, young professionals are starting to face what the New York Times calls an "AI Job Apocalypse."[45]

To be honest, I can see this coming. I recently became an AI entrepreneur because I see how AI could help to address long-lasting issues with regulation and regulatory reforms—we will talk about them soon in the next chapter.

As I set up my GovTech startup, with dreams and expectations for growth, labor-wise, I know that I will not be eliminating existing jobs, but I will most likely not create jobs that would have been needed years ago.

AI is not to blame for all this. It is only a tool. A tool developed and used by humans. Some of these humans are trying to do good. Many others are looking to make a profit. Others are aiming for both. This is entirely okay if we agree to play and live under the market economy rules most countries follow.

However, as a government leader responsible for pursuing and protecting the public good, you will have to decide between creating an environment where AI grows to serve humans, versus letting AI grow at the expense of humans, including their jobs.

My guess is that this dilemma will reach you sooner rather than later.

I want to close this chapter by saying that more issues will arise from AI's use, and it will be difficult to keep track of everything. A good recent initiative comes *from MIT and its AI Risk Repository.* It is currently a living database of 1,000+ AI risks with causal and domain taxonomy. I invite you to learn about it.

Key messages to remember

- Part of AI's disruption is that it can, or already is, taking over tasks usually done by less skilled or less experienced workers.
- As this dynamic evolves and increases, your government will have to decide what to do about desirable public goods, such as people being employed and having a good enough source of income.

Use AI to Create Better AI Regulation

"Significant attention has been paid of late on how best to approach potential regulation of artificial intelligence (AI). But what about the converse of this proposition—how can AI help governments become more efficient in issuing and analyzing regulations?"

—Dan Chenok and Virginia Huth

love the quote above. Discussions about what to regulate in AI will grow and become as complex as possible. Remember the pacing problem I mentioned in the first chapters? It will also add to the factors constraining your capacity to steer and get AI regulation right in your country.

But wait a minute. AI is supposed to make things easier, helping people become more productive and do things that would take an entire village to achieve, right?

What if AI can help your government have better regulations?

When asking this, I have in mind how AI can assist you in implementing Chapter 4, or, as I have been calling it, the "how" to better regulate AI.

Then, why not use AI to also improve all the regulations in your country, something very costly and close to impossible nowadays?

I founded a GovTech startup with this vision in mind. I invite you to learn more about "fAIrly simple" at https://fairlysimple.io/.

In the meantime, in this brief chapter, I will share a few ideas we will be working on to help governments and leaders worldwide use AI to improve regulation, so they can achieve better policy results.

Make Your Regulations More Accessible and Easier to Understand

My wife was shocked. She is a lawyer educated in Mexico and the United States. In both countries, you usually need a legal background to understand laws and regulations, but you most certainly do not need one to go online and find a specific government law or regulation.

She was very surprised when I told her about my findings from a regulatory predictability diagnostic I did in Ethiopia. In sum, their Official Gazette did not have an online presence. Major laws (proclamations) were available only as scanned versions of the hard copies. On top of that, they were scattered across multiple government websites.

What struck her most was the story that a former judicial-sector lawyer told me. The lawyer said that early in his public-sector career, it was not rare to have to pay if you wanted access to the law, the actual legal text only available on paper. Yes, even if the lawyer was part of the government!

I did not want to tell her stories from private sector representatives. Several mentioned that it was common for government officials speaking with firms to suddenly take out, from a drawer, a circular or letter nobody knew about, but that had significant requirements and implications for their businesses.

This practice is not unique to Ethiopia. Even when I worked in Malaysia, a more advanced economy aiming to reach high-income status, the issue of access to regulatory information was real. It exists in many countries.

Even though many experts and a few governments aim for a central portal that unifies and gives access to all laws and regulations, things should go beyond this significant and desirable goal.

As a government leader, you should remember that SMEs, individual entrepreneurs, investors—foreign and local—and citizens in general do not want to become experts to read and understand the law.

Rather, they want to grasp, in simple language, the rules that apply to their business and how to comply with them.

Just as PEMUDAH says, "no more regulation than necessary," a good goal to aim for is: *"no more time than necessary to access and understand laws and regulations."*

Government-made rules should be accessible to everyone, so people and businesses do not have to spend time getting tangled up in, and then untangled from, understanding and navigating regulatory requirements.

Luckily, AI is here and has the potential to make regulatory information available to everyone in a user-friendly way. In the language people use every day. No legal expertise needed.

Stakeholder Feedback and Quality Control Checks

I mentioned predictability earlier. It is part of the name of the game when you want to improve your country's regulations.

Many government leaders do not understand how unpredictable regulation hinders their ability to achieve better economic and policy results. Or, in some cases, they know it but do not want to pay the price of fixing it.

Predictability is not for every type of government leader. Especially the archetypal political leader who sells change without changing anything, or those who are afraid of opening up and acting differently, like authentically listening to the public to make better decisions.

Not everyone can be that type of leader. My work supporting governments with national public consultation platforms proved it.

I love the opportunities that technology brings to close the gap between governments and citizens. It has been part of my international development career, starting when the hype was about SMS-enabled citizen engagement, until I helped governments with the conceptual design of national public consultation portals to gather feedback and comments on proposed regulations.

However, after several years of experience in this subfield, I have built the reluctance expressed a few lines above, regarding leadership. The problem has never been technology. It will never be.

Nonetheless, my enthusiasm remains very high for what AI can do to improve and facilitate how governments conduct public consultation on new rules before they are approved, from making regulatory proposals more accessible to the general public, letting people ask questions about them, and of course, allowing governments to analyze and respond to these questions and comments, as well as identify inconsistencies between proposed regulations and existing rules.

There is so much you can do with technology. You can pilot this with your AI regulations. Just remember, AI is a tool. The underlying problems and principles remain the same. In this case, go back to Chapter 4 to not lose perspective on this.

Cut Red Tape and Simplify Everyone's Life

Certainty that comes from predictable rules matters a lot. But bad regulations can also be very predictable. They can be predictably awful.

As legal mandates and requirements trickle down from laws, to regulations to licensing and administrative procedures, things can get ugly for citizens, businesses and everyone.

Maybe your regulations on starting a business are pretty decent. But who said that to get a business license, one needs to submit three hard copies of documents rubber-stamped in green ink, only between 9:30 and 11:30 a.m., otherwise it is not going to happen!

It sounds ridiculous, right? However, that is often the reality many citizens and businesses must deal with every single time they interact with their government.

In Chapter 4, I talked about the importance of simplifying your AI regulation first, and only then going digital to facilitate compliance with related administrative requirements. Sure, it is easier said than done. This is where AI might help you.

From an ex-ante perspective, AI can help your government cut red tape before it becomes a problem. In other words, it can help you to understand whether the rubber stamp in green ink is necessary, whether the requirements you are about to impose contradict or duplicate those from other rules, and even whether you already have that information and do not have to ask for it twice.

I know governments can certainly do all this, too. The challenge is scaling these efforts up.

These AI-assisted actions can also help with upcoming AI regulations that introduce new requirements and obligations.

From an ex-post perspective, AI can be a great tool for analyzing what already exists. That is the topic of the section below. So, let's jump into that discussion.

Analyze and Reform Large Volumes of Regulation

When I started working on regulatory issues, I found it difficult to understand why experts and advisors placed a great emphasis on getting RIA right.

Yes, regulatory proposals based on evidence are a great thing to aim for. Yet, in the countries where I have worked, I have seen governments spending so much energy, time and resources to get RIA right, while leaving unaddressed other big issues like reviewing and fixing existing regulations; the rules that are hitting people and firms in the country straight and hard.

As I mentioned before, there are two reasons to explain this.

A greater emphasis on RIA makes a lot of sense when your regulatory framework is more or less good. RIA prevents noise, pollution or however you want to call bad regulation, from entering the system. That is what advanced economies do.

However, for those countries without an adequate regulatory environment, the priority should be to fix the thousands of existing bad regulations, like the rules killing private-sector development and holding your government back from achieving better policy results.

Why is this not happening? Well, it is not easy. It requires technical capacity. Even if you have capable teams, it is an issue of numbers. Numbers related to the budget envelope, the amount of time and staff you need to review thousands of rules in your regulatory system. Thousands of regulations with trillions and trillions of words someone will have to read!

If you have tried to review and reform regulations, you know how hard it can be. What about reviewing rules affecting trade, investment or your entire economy? Almost impossible, right? Well, not now, with AI.

At fAIrly simple, part of the vision is to *"reform smarter, not harder."*

We say this because we believe in AI solutions to review large volumes of regulation without you having to break the bank, hire thousands of lawyers and experts you cannot always afford, spend years in this process, or get suboptimal results from AI tools not specialized on regulation.

Enforce Rules More Effectively

To close this chapter on what AI can do to improve "how" you regulate AI and other domains, I want to touch on something I alluded to in Chapter 4.

Your government can have the best rules in place, but without compliance, those regulations become useless.

What do governments usually do to implement rules? They conduct inspections to monitor compliance. Sometimes, they have enforcement mechanisms. But all this requires human and financial resources that are scarce.

This has led to new solutions, such as the risk-based and outcome-based regulations I discussed in Chapter 5. Also, some governments have explored behavioral nudges when designing and implementing rules.

Again, now we have AI. Artificial Intelligence can help your government design and implement interventions like the ones I just mentioned. Or it can even assist with, and perform, some of the monitoring activities that government inspectors do.

For example, on construction sites, drones can help verify compliance with important safety rules. Even simple cameras powered with the right AI algorithm can be used to monitor how long a car has been parked in a specific spot, illegal land use and many more things you can think about—as my friend and colleague Shashank Jayakumar does at his company, Yotaka Solutions.

Key messages to remember

- Actively managing the lifecycle of AI regulation or regulation in general is not an easy task for governments.
- AI has now opened the door to implement many regulatory practices and reforms in an easier and faster way so you can reform smarter, not harder.
- Explore how you can leverage AI within your government. I am also happy to help you, if I can.

Part III

How to Succeed Without Getting Lost

Creating and improving AI regulations is not an easy task, especially when you approach this from a government-wide perspective. There are so many things that can derail your best policies, including your government's AI Regulatory Policy.

In Part 3, I will share a few things you need to address to improve your chances of achieving better AI regulations. I will touch on the institutions that need to be part of this, including their roles and how you should support them. I will also allude to some of the invisible factors that "kill" policy implementation in domains that affect and touch all corners of government.

Finally, I will share a visual tool to brainstorm and bring together many things covered in the book, so you can have a space to collaborate, ideate and strategize with your teams. I call this tool the "BRAIn Canvas."

Someone Needs to Take Care of All This

"Nothing is possible without men, but nothing lasts without institutions."

—Jean Monnet

"Forging and adopting technically sound policies is necessary for successful development, but it is not enough: any policy is only as good as its implementation... But without a supporting institutional framework and capable public sector organizations to implement them, even technically sound policies and programs are likely to fail."

—Loayza and Woolcock

In Part 2, we went over the "how" to regulate AI, and then we touched on "what" to regulate—either to promote AI's growth or protect us from it.

As a government leader, you may be asking yourself—or me as the author—"who" is going to be doing all of this work?

Who is going to create and coordinate the AI regulatory sandboxes? Who is going to monitor biases in AI algorithms? Who is going to lead government efforts to build the necessary AI digital infrastructure that touches on multiple things like investment, trade, electricity, water and reliable internet? Who is going to help different regulators and make sure they follow the proper "how" to regulate process covered in Chapter 4? The list of "who" just goes on.

This is a great moment to rewind and recap some of the things I said in Chapter 3. I will quote myself:

"You need an institution that leads and coordinates AI regulation across government. The coordination part is extremely important."

The next chapter will be about coordination and the pains you have to address when implementing your better AI regulation plan, policy or agenda. In this chapter, I will talk about the institution that leads and guides others in this effort.

Despite having different names, like Good Regulatory Practices, Better Regulation, Regulatory Improvement or Management, I chose Regulatory Policy or **AI Regulatory Policy** for the *"Overlooked Policy Framework Governments and Policymakers Need to Regulate an AI-Driven World,"* alluded to in the book's subtitle.

Why? I said that this name gives this agenda the explicit recognition and status of public policy, just like other policies, such as health, fiscal, national security, energy, environmental and more.

As a government leader, can you conceive any of these policies succeeding without a dedicated institution or set of institutions supporting their goals? It would be weird, right?

I am sure that you will say or think that the institution, per se, is not enough. It needs an appropriate mandate to operate, collaborate and interact with other government institutions. It needs the necessary staff, budget and other resources to deliver on its mandate and policy objectives. Of course, it needs political support from the center of government.

Without an institution and all these supporting elements, your AI Regulatory Policy about the "how" and "what" to regulate is destined to fail. Let me be more specific: it may already be dead before it comes to life.

But do not get disappointed or less motivated. Some people say that "death is just the beginning." So, if your country's regulatory policy is buried five meters below ground, remember that AI regulation is your new opportunity to get things right.

So, let's talk about the things you need to know about the institution(s) leading your government's AI Regulatory Policy. Let's talk about the "who" that will take care of most things we have discussed so far.

The Institution(s) Leading the Way

In the image below, you will see the key elements of an AI Regulatory Policy from an institutional angle. This is an adaptation of what I shared in Chapter 2, when I talked about regulatory policy.

Key Elements of an AI Regulatory Policy

A government-wide policy that applies to all AI regulations

Led by an institution that coordinates its implementation and supports AI regulators to:

Better manage the lifecycle of their AI regulations through a process that relies on a set of:

Good Regulatory Practices that bring transparency, predictability, participation and the use of evidence to AI regulatory decisions.

From this, we can quickly infer that your *government-wide AI Regulatory Policy,* the one that brings order to the "how" or the process to actively manage your AI regulations, needs an institution to lead, coordinate and support its implementation.

Remember that, to succeed, every policy needs an institution to lead the way. I will reinforce this message with words from the quote at the beginning of the chapter, from Loayza and Woolcock at the World Bank:

"… without a supporting institutional framework and capable public sector organizations to implement them, even technically sound policies and programs are likely to fail."[46]

I hope the message went through. You may have more questions, like: What is that institution supposed to do? Where in the entire administration should it sit? Should it be a new institution or part of an existing one?

Well, you are part of a government or planning to join one. So, you know or should know that these institutional decisions are more of an art than an exact science. They must be tailored to the peculiarities of your country. Nonetheless, I will give you my two cents, based on what I have seen in many countries trying to implement a national regulatory policy.

Let's start with the last question: Should your government create a new institution, or can your AI Regulatory Policy fall within the mandate of an existing one?

My advice goes in two directions. If you already have a good track record and capacity to regulate well, in general, find an existing institution that is already leading and coordinating regulatory efforts across your government. Once you choose this path, it is important to build the knowledge and capacity of that institution to take on new and constantly evolving topics like AI and future innovations.

If your government is not good at regulation and you do not have a solid institution to support and coordinate effective regulatory practices across government, then your country may be a good candidate to create an agency dedicated to dealing with AI regulation, and possibly other AI topics that your government needs to steer. It could be an AI National Agency, AI National Commission or Council.

Of course, there is always the temptation to nest this agenda in your ministry or agency for digital transformation or ICT. Because I do not know the specifics of your government, that may be a possibility. However, AI is very different from traditional ICTs, and the approach and skills required might not be the same as what you already have.

Again, these are my two cents, without knowing the specifics of your country's public administration. But addressing the next question can give you more clarity. So, let's talk briefly about where in the public administration this agency, institution or group should sit.

Let me start with a simple analogy on how regulatory policy efforts are led in some countries. This agenda is sometimes nested within ministries of trade, due to the natural relevance of regulation to technical barriers; public administration or planning because regulation is a government function and tool to achieve public policy objectives; justice, when only looking at the legal aspect of regulations; or in specific commissions, councils or agencies that deal with productivity, investment and competitiveness because regulation highly influences all of them.

While any of these options might work, in practice, there is always a struggle for this agenda to take off and function adequately: *these institutions have the same or less power and independence than their peers within government.*

Because regulatory policy, and most importantly, *your AI Regulatory Policy,* needs an institution to lead, coordinate and often impose obligations across all or most government agencies, you can imagine the power struggles and turf battles between the leading AI agency and the rest of the government.

I have witnessed it, and you surely know that this can easily become an energy-consuming and frustrating role, especially when you do not have the right mandate, resources, tools and support to do it.

What is an alternative? If your government considers AI regulation and AI matters a real priority, then this agenda should be at the center of government or very close to it, assuming this is a place capable of driving change across government.

From there, you can start with a small team, building the foundations for an AI national strategy that includes AI regulation. Then, you should aim to nurture and support this small beginning until it is ready to spin off as an independent body with its own mandate and resources.

Again, these are my two cents from what I have seen in several countries. You know your country and public administration better. Having said that, there is a final element that is equally important to the "who" is leading your AI regulatory policy: the functions this institution should perform.

Let me start by saying that if you create an AI national agency, commission or body, it would probably have responsibilities beyond regulation. Below, I will focus on the functions that will help you implement an AI Regulatory Policy in your country, regardless of who is leading it.

1. **Create awareness.** For starters, you need to acknowledge that AI and innovation are often alien to regulatory and public officials in your government. As a first step, you need to create awareness about AI internally. This includes its benefits, challenges, and, of course, policy and regulatory implications. A second step is raising awareness about the "how" and "what" to regulate, so your agencies have the right tools and are better positioned to implement this agenda.

2. **Build capacity.** Implementing the "how" and "what" to regulate AI comes with tasks and responsibilities that many of your regulatory agencies and staff are not used to. So, help them on this journey with training, staff, guidelines and adequate resources. As we will discuss soon, they hold the key to your AI regulatory policy. If they do not implement your policy, you are not going anywhere.

3. **Coordination.** There is a reason I am dedicating the next chapter to this topic. By now, you can probably see why. Your AI regulatory policy will require strength, patience and strategic thinking to perform this key function.

4. **Identify areas for reform.** The institution leading your AI Regulatory Policy will not necessarily implement reforms, but it can play a key role in identifying where policy and regulatory reforms are needed.

5. **Monitor progress.** This is a powerful yet overlooked function. It first requires keeping track of the agencies that are implementing the AI Regulatory Policy, whether it is mandatory or not. Then, the second and more important part is to benchmark and make their performance

public. This creates positive peer pressure and competition that comes from seeing yourself at the top, middle or bottom of the pack.

The Institutions Ultimately Implementing the "How" and "What"

A few lines above, I mentioned that regulatory agencies and their staff hold the key to your AI regulatory policy.

You can have a great institution leading, coordinating and supporting the way. However, line ministries and regulators are ultimately responsible for creating and managing rules within their mandates.

That is why it is important for your government to support them. Remember, much of this is new to all of them, and they are probably already working under limited resources.

So, do not do what other countries have done—creating wonderful, better-regulation laws with lots of new obligations to improve the quality of regulation, yet asking agencies to do all of that without extra budget allocations.

My friend and peer, Cesar Cordova, says it very well: *"You cannot have better regulations without better regulators."* I will use his wisdom to tell you that you *cannot have better AI regulations without better AI regulators.*

The Institution Letting This Happen

There is an important reason I suggested nesting your AI regulatory policy and institution at the center of government.

I have witnessed several times a story that goes like this: a great technical regulatory policy team—usually small, sometimes a little larger—works super hard to improve regulations in the country and deliver the impossible with very few resources they have, only to suddenly hit the wall because the center of government does not believe in this agenda.

There is only so much you can do when important public policies like this are dominated by political ideologies, interests and fears. Dead end. No escape from that place.

However, I will say it again. Success in the AI regulation field will not be achieved by the prototypical leader who leans more toward the political side of things than toward policy solutions.

This agenda is not for someone who is afraid of "losing micro-management control" to let others work, collaborate, shine and do the right thing.

I will close this idea, section and chapter with a quote from Tony Blair, an international leader who thought differently and said that policy goes first, politics second:[47]

"… decide the right policy to solve the problem, and then fashion the right politics around it; don't decide on the politics and then form a policy to suit."

Key messages to remember

- As with any public policy, your AI Regulatory Policy needs an institution or set of institutions to lead the way. Make sure that institution has enough resources to do so.
- Regulators are ultimately responsible for implementing your AI Regulatory Policy. This will be new for many of them, so make sure they receive the support they need to succeed.
- The center of government plays a key role in letting all of this happen. If you are there and you believe in this agenda, do not let politics win the battle. Policy goes first.

9
Coordinate, Coordinate, and "Kill the Killers"

"Joined-up government is based on the view that public policy goals cannot be met through the separate activities of existing organizations, nor can they be delivered by grouping several departments under a common agency... To join up, initiatives must align organizations with different cultures, incentives, management systems and aims, and they must align governments to citizens and their needs. The keys are sharing and coordination of information across boundaries to integrate policies and activities."

—Williams, Gravesen and Brownhill

I have said it several times throughout the book: coordination is very important for your AI Regulatory Policy's success.

As opposed to other public policies like health, education or agriculture, which are more vertical than horizontal, your AI Regulatory Policy is or will be, almost as horizontal as it can get.

The more AI advances and is widely used, the more it will fall under the mandate and governance of different ministries, departments and agencies. This includes AI's use in health, education, agriculture, law enforcement or public services.

All these agencies with regulatory powers will have to regulate AI sooner or later when its use falls within their domain.

On top of that, subnational governments—as they are already doing in some countries—will also be regulating AI aspects within their turf and legal control.

You do not need to be a fortune teller to envision how this can end. It is very likely that you already know or have witnessed this dynamic: *a situation in which everyone issues regulations at their own will, on things that are under their scope of power. The overall result is an absolutely uncoordinated mess.*

The initial policy rationale behind the proposed AI regulation moratorium at the state level in the United States in 2025 had this concern in mind. While in many countries final decisions are often more political, it is important to understand that without a national framework for AI and AI regulation, new rules will flow from left, right and center, creating an absolute regulatory mess that will indeed hinder innovation, while leaving desirable public goods un-protected and at risk.

Therefore, in addition to the "how," "what," and "who," *coordination* should be another name of the game in the space of AI regulation.

So, let's start talking about what you, as a government leader, can strategically do to incentivize coordination in a siloed and fragmented bureaucracy, as your entire government may be.

Interagency Consultations

My first impressions of intergovernmental coordination in regulation came from my early work on public consultation or notice-and-comment procedures.

At that time, the goal was to help governments use digital tools to announce regulatory proposals, receive stakeholder feedback and comments, and then publicly respond to participation and comments received, similarly to what I mentioned in Chapter 4 in the section on "Procedural Fairness in Action," and Chapter 7 in the section on "Stakeholder Feedback and Quality Control Checks."

However, after talking to business associations and regulators in a few countries, it became clear that before reaching the stage of public consultations on regulatory proposals, there had to be a previous step: *an internal consultation among government agencies.*

The purpose? To have a quality check point or filter to address traditional conflicts like overlaps, contradictions and duplications of mandate that new regulations often create.

How? First, this should be part of the requirements in your AI Regulatory Policy, so regulators need to go through this step in the rulemaking process (see the diagram below).

Then, you need to implement this requirement through your public consultation platform. If you do not have one, build and launch one. There are 40-plus countries worldwide that have already done it.

This is the advice my colleagues and I gave governments asking for support to build a national public consultation portal:

"You have or will have the digital tool to run public consultations, but that does not limit yourself to do other types of non-public and necessary consultations, like an interagency consultation on your proposed regulations."

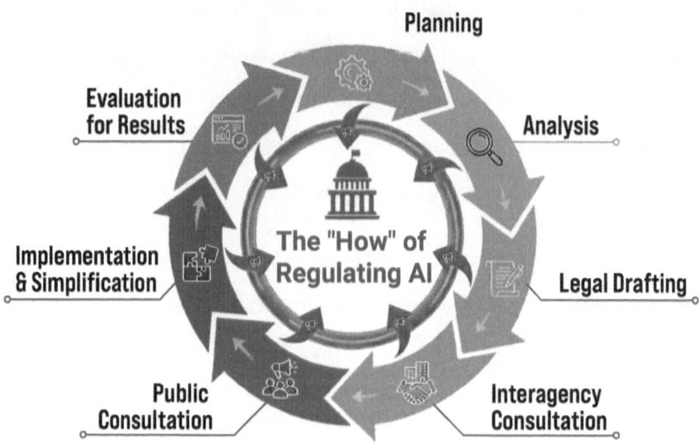

Interagency consultations should apply to AI rules, too. If you already have a national platform to do public consultation on regulatory proposals, use it to consult on AI regulation. Then, explore how to run non-public interagency consultations on an AI regulatory proposal for coordination purposes.

If you still do not have a public consultation portal, build one with that idea in mind. The tool will be there. Getting the most out of it depends more on your versatility and strategic thinking. It will be like scoring twice with a single shot.

Coordination Also Starts with Planning

I like to think and help create digital solutions that solve traditional and un-resolved regulatory issues. Using technology makes a lot of sense most of the time. However, I recognize that not everything has to be a tech solution. There are different ways to achieve the same goal.

In the field of government coordination to improve AI regulatory outcomes, I want to return to something I mentioned at the beginning of Chapter 4, when I went over some quick lessons on "how" to regulate AI.

Does the phrase *"everything starts with planning"* ring a bell? Yes, planning and announcing AI regulatory changes is not only the beginning of your regulatory process or cycle. It is also the crucial moment where coordination with other government agencies should start.

How? First, give your AI regulatory plan a real chance. By this, I mean you have to implement it. Keep it simple, but do it and make it mandatory.

Then, observe the dynamics that come from publicly announcing regulatory changes in advance, before any text is even drafted.

From a bureaucratic perspective, this may sound like additional internal burdens on already overworked regulators. Politically, it may be viewed as a simple way to "unnecessarily" stir up the hornet's nest within your troops.

From a strategic leadership perspective, it is the way to incentivize change.

In addition to external transparency and predictability, your AI regulatory agenda will create internal transparency within your government. There will be no excuses or space for AI regulatory decisions that nobody, or very few, within government knew about.

If you are at the center of government, you may think that everything is under your control, because everything passes through you, and that is the way it should be.

Right. But this is a different approach in which you, at the center, let go of some of that control and let the "market" of different government agencies check on each other.

Less exhausting? Probably. Also, potentially more effective because government agencies will have more opportunities to see what other agencies are proposing, react in time and influence the consistency of those decisions before they go public.

The beauty of this is that you are not prescribing government coordination through your AI regulatory plan—though you can still do that if you want.

Rather, you are creating opportunities and space for coordination to happen more organically at a very early stage of your AI regulatory process.

Of course, this requires a change of mindset. The demand from the center of government is to let go of some central control, so others can shine and do their part. It means becoming the leader who does everything for their team to excel and shine—not the other way around.

In the book's last chapter, we will talk about some of these mindset changes. For now, start thinking about your AI regulatory plan as an opportunity to score twice in a single shot, and create a space for agencies to react and, at some point, learn on their own how to coordinate.

Ad Hoc Commissions, Committees, Councils, Bodies and Working Groups

This section goes back to the "who" rather than to an actual mechanism for coordination. Nonetheless, it is important to consider it.

In the last chapter, when I shared the idea that an institution had to lead and coordinate the implementation of your AI Regulatory Policy, I had in mind a single dedicated institution—an AI National Agency, AI National Commission or Council—responsible, among other things, for AI regulation.

However, on several occasions, I alluded to the idea of a single institution or set of institutions leading this agenda. That idea came from what I have seen many governments do.

They create interministerial or interagency commissions, committees, councils, bodies or working groups to coordinate a specific topic or regulatory field.

For instance, institutions implementing policies to promote investment, trade, competitiveness and productivity all have to deal with improving business regulation to achieve those policy goals at some point. They know coordination is crucial, to say the least.

For example, in the United States, the Small Business Administration (SBA) has an Office of Advocacy that plays a very important role in influencing and coordinating government regulations that affect SMEs. The SBA is one of the "who" in the United States.

How do they do their part? Just as we said in the section above, they monitor and review regulatory proposals with potential impact on small businesses before the rules are even proposed. From the very early stage of planning.

If a proposed rule raises significant concerns about its impact on SMEs, the SBA communicates with regulators, raises an alert, gathers feedback from stakeholders, and ultimately submits formal comments to the regulatory agency in question.

From this, you can start thinking that as AI regulation increases in volume and scope in your country, you may eventually need these types of groups to coordinate AI regulation on specific aspects.

If you decide to create your AI National Agency, AI National Commission, or AI Council, it goes without saying that all these bodies will have to coordinate with or even be structurally linked to this AI national body.

"Kill the Killers"

I heard this phrase when I was with the World Bank. At that time, my Vice President was Felipe Jaramillo. My few interactions with him gave me the impression that he liked to keep things simple.

"Kill the killers" was his way of transmitting the message to get rid of the internal red tape and bureaucracy that really slowed the World Bank's response to government clients' needs for advisory services and financial support.

His phrase made a good impression and has stayed with me since then. It perfectly applies to government bureaucracies and how they perform key policy functions like regulation.

What does this mean for AI regulation and your AI regulatory policy?

I have talked about several of those "killers" throughout the book. Here, I will briefly recapitulate them and mention a few more. To do so, I need to reiterate that even the best-designed policy, including your AI Regulatory Policy, can fail due to poor implementation.

This happened in my home country, Mexico. At some point, it had a comprehensive national law to improve regulations. A very good one. But without sufficient resources to implement it, as well as changes in administration and priorities, the initial comprehensive and well-designed policy slowly died.

Among the things you can do to "kill the killers" that could take your AI Regulatory Policy to the grave, are:

- **Allocate necessary resources.** I already mentioned that you cannot conceive a successful policy without adequate human, financial and material resources. This has been a big mistake many governments have made. As my friend and international expert on regulatory reforms, Cesar Cordova says, "You cannot expect regulatory quality for free." If you want good AI regulation, you need to invest in it.
- **Build the capacity of regulatory agencies.** Remember, the "how" to regulate and the "what" to regulate are new for your regulators. How do people react—especially in bureaucracies—when they have to do new things, have not done those new things before and have little knowledge about them? Build their capacity to create better AI regulations.
- **Create the right incentives.** In siloed and bureaucratic organizations, it is not enough to have the right resources and knowledge. The real-life struggles go beyond that, and touch on managing people, incentives, and competing interests. If you are in a leadership position, you will have to plan for the right incentives—either sticks, carrots or nudges—to let your AI Regulatory Policy implementation flow more naturally. This is extremely context-specific, and you are in a better position to find the right approach. Nonetheless, you need to plan for it.

- **Pick the political battles that are worth fighting.** You may know that many policies fail because they do not have the right support from the center of government. We already covered this. Regulating is a way to exercise power. When you constrain the discretion on "how" you regulate, you limit that power. Still, there are some battles that are worth fighting, whether you lead a country, ministry, agency, department or team. Fight those worthy battles and remember Tony Blair's advice: get the policy right first and then sort out the politics needed to make it happen.

There is a fifth point I want to share, but it is the content of the last chapter. It is about the concept of "regulatory humility" that I have mentioned, and most importantly, about changing the only thing that is always under your control and power to change: You!

We will get to that idea soon.

Key messages to remember

- Coordination within government is crucial for the successful implementation of your AI Regulatory Policy.
- It can happen in many ways and at many moments.
- There are many things that will silently undermine your efforts. Remember to "kill the killers" of your policy implementation and pick the battles that are worth fighting for.

10

Use Your BRAIn Canvas

"Crafting a business model is no different. Ideas placed in the Canvas trigger new ones. The Canvas becomes a tool for facilitating the idea dialogue—for individuals sketching out their ideas and for groups developing ideas together."

—Alexander Osterwalder

I have told you a lot of things so far. My intention has been to share a strategic vision on AI regulation, so you can then go deeper on your own or with the help of local and international experts, including myself.

You can always revisit the different chapters and sections in this book. However, at some point, it is useful to have a visual tool that puts things together and helps you and your teams brainstorm, organize ideas and develop government strategies and plans for AI regulation in your country.

A tool like that for the private sector is the Business Model Canvas by Alexander Osterwalder. Many entrepreneurs are very familiar with it. Super useful. As a

GovTech business starter, I have benefited from the Business Model and Value Proposition Canvases.

My first interaction with it was during my work with Keith McLean, friend and international governance expert. We were supporting a group of young leaders to take ownership of a global anti-corruption network incubated by the World Bank. It was not a for-profit initiative, but the goal was to find a business model that could make the global network sustainable without international aid.

We held a workshop in Istanbul with the help of Michael Lachapelle and Doug Morwood, senior experts in business model innovation and fantastic guys. I still remember the room with the large printouts, multiple-color Post-it notes on the windows, walls and the Business Model Canvas itself.

If you are reluctant about workshops where you need to talk a lot, participate, collaborate and report back on group discussions, I hear you. Some people thrive in those settings. Others feel uncomfortable, uninterested or neutral.

However, I invite you to think about the space for collaboration and exchange of ideas that a Canvas creates. How you decide to implement it—small setting, large gathering, out-of-office retreat, previous homework, etc.—is up to you.

Having said all of that, in this chapter, I want to provide you with a visual tool like the Business Model Canvas is for the private sector: a tool to map, visualize and start discussing the different elements related to AI regulation in your country and government—several of which we have covered in the previous chapters.

I call this tool the **B**etter **R**egulation of **A**rtificial **In**telligence Canvas, or simply the *BRAIn Canvas.*

The BRAIn Canvas is a high-level strategic tool for government leaders and policymakers like you to map, analyze and improve AI regulation in your country and organization.

BRAIn Canvas

A high-level strategic tool for government leaders, policy-makers and their teams to brainstorm, map and plan on how to improve AI regulations.

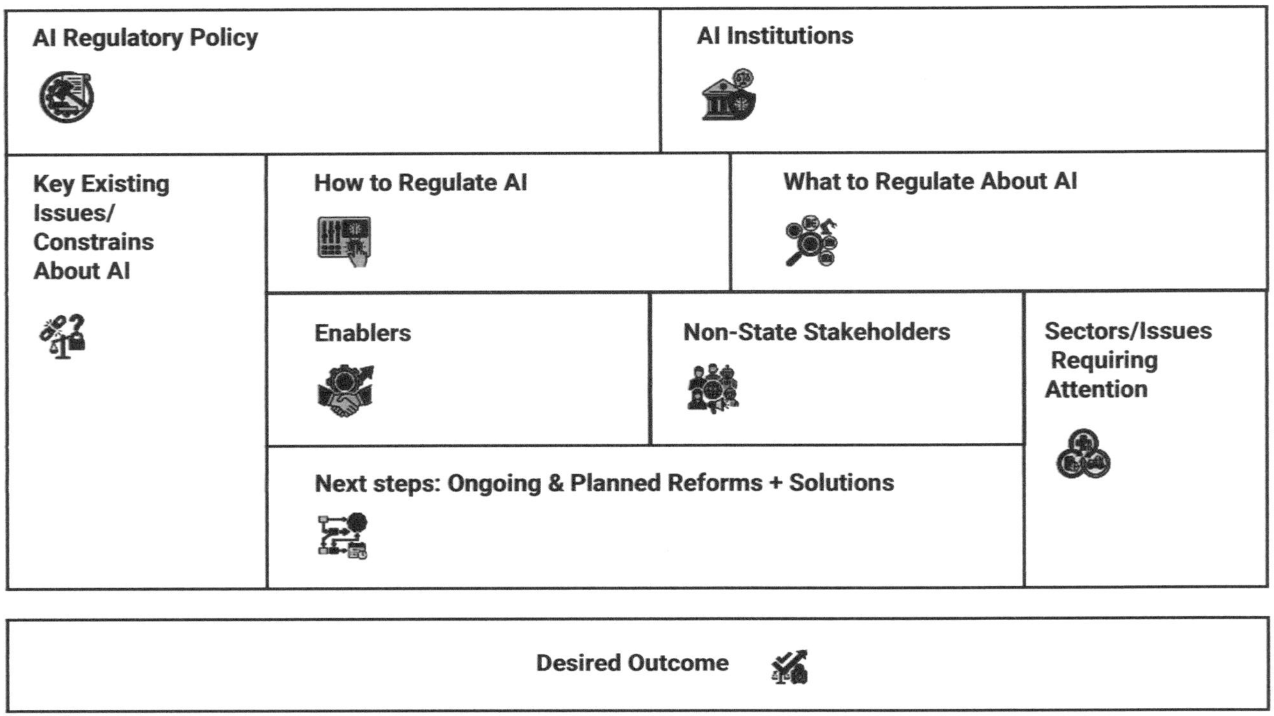

AI Regulatory Policy

AI Institutions

Key Existing Issues/ Constrains About AI

How to Regulate AI

What to Regulate About AI

Enablers

Non-State Stakeholders

Sectors/Issues Requiring Attention

Next steps: Ongoing & Planned Reforms + Solutions

Desired Outcome 

The BRAIn Canvas Itself

There is no better way to gain practical knowledge of a tool than to become familiar with it and then get your feet wet using it.

Above, you will see what the BRAIn Canvas looks like. Shortly, I will describe and elaborate on each of the boxes or elements comprising the Canvas. But let me start with a general description.

At the top, the BRAIn Canvas touches on the building block of your AI Regulatory Policy and the "who" to support its implementation—we covered this in Chapters 3 and 8.

Below, it aims to map the "how" and "what" to regulate about AI—the content of Chapters 4, 5 and 6.

On the sides—vertically—the Canvas will help you put together context-specific issues related to AI in your country.

In the middle, the idea is for you to map enablers (current and future) as well as relevant involvement of non-state actors in AI regulation—some of those enablers were mentioned in Chapters 7 and 9, and throughout the book.

At the bottom, the BRAIn Canvas aims to capture your ongoing and planned efforts, or reforms, to improve AI regulation through a more strategic and systematic approach.

Finally, below everything is the starting point for your BRAIn Canvas. It is your expected outcome from both having an AI Regulator Policy and engaging in this type of strategic policy analysis to get there.

Let's take a closer look at each of these elements so you can get a better idea of what they include.

Your AI Regulatory Policy and Institutions

AI Regulatory Policy	AI Institutions

The titles might look self-explanatory, and indeed they are. In the first box, the idea is for you to map whether or not you have an **AI Regulatory Policy** and an **AI Institution** leading and coordinating its implementation.

However, practice is more nuanced than a yes-or-no answer. Thus, even if you do not have an AI Regulatory Policy, in that section of the BRAIn Canvas, you can add the existing elements that may lead or support your future AI Regulatory Policy. This includes current laws, regulations, policies and guidelines in your legal and policy frameworks.

Even if you already have an AI Regulatory Policy, include all the legal and policy instruments linked to it here.

The same goes for your AI Institution(s). If you have one or more, include them there. Otherwise, add the names of relevant institutions that may take on a larger role once you start designing your plan to approach AI regulation more strategically.

Remember, there are no right or wrong answers for the content in these Canvas boxes. What really matters are the ideas, discussions, and collaboration within your team or group that will emerge as you start filling those sections with Post-it, text or however you decide to do it—more on that later.

The "How" and "What" to Regulate AI in Your Country

How to Regulate AI	What to Regulate About AI

This is all about Part 2. We discussed a lot there, so there may be many things to map in these two Canvas sections.

On the *"how"* to regulate, identify whether your government is already doing some of the things covered in Chapter 4, even if not necessarily for AI regulation.

The idea is to identify initiatives and practices you can build on. If you really have nothing, leave notes on things that make sense to start doing, from both a strategic and practical perspective.

On the *"what"* to regulate, remember that these are the things you might regulate about AI, not because others are doing it, or because it is trendy worldwide. Everything starts with a problem. Thus, if you have already regulated AI, include those "what" items here. If you plan to do so, make sure those future regulations respond to an actual problem. Finally, it is a good idea to differentiate between regulations that enable AI's growth and regulations that protect us from AI—like in Chapters 5 and 6.

Issues That Require Your Attention

Key Existing Issues/ Constrains About AI

Sectors/Issues Requiring Attention

In this part of the BRAIn Canvas, you will map the important things that are happening around AI in your country.

First, you have a section on *Key Existing Issues.* Some may already have a regulatory response in place or in the pipeline. Many more may remain unaddressed or just be emerging. The idea here is for you to identify the challenges your country faces with AI's adoption.

In the *Sectors Requiring Attention,* you can add the sectors, industries or activities where action is already needed. These are issues that should move quickly into the "what" and "how," if you decide that AI regulation is the best approach to address the problems in question.

Even when no regulatory action is needed, this section of the BRAIn Canvas will help you keep an eye on strategic areas, for instance, data center infrastructure, or unintended labor or discrimination issues arising from AI's use.

Enablers and Non-State Actors

Enablers	Non-State Stakeholders

In the *Enablers for AI Regulation* box, you can include things your government has done or can do to create and implement a sound AI Regulatory Policy, as well as improve the quality of AI regulation.

Examples of enablers might include strong technical capacity in your regulatory agencies, good availability of data for policy design, or maybe a digital platform that already supports one of the steps in the AI regulatory process. Of course, political support and prioritization, as well as active think tanks and policy or research centers, are also enablers that can contribute to better AI regulations.

Then, consider that not everything on this agenda falls on the government side. In the *Non-State Actors* section, add what the private sector, academic, NGOs, donors and other organizations are doing and planning to do to influence AI regulation. Here, it is not only about the "who" but also about going deeper into the "what" they are doing and "why."

Ongoing and Planned Reforms to Improve AI Regulation and Your AI Regulatory Policy

Next steps: Ongoing & Planned Reforms + Solutions

Finally, the last section of the Canvas is for you to map and identify your government's initiatives and reforms to improve AI regulation.

It could include individual measures—this or that AI regulation. But the main point here is to capture strategic and whole-of-government initiatives that improve AI regulations systematically, not one at a time.

Some of these ongoing or planned initiatives will also appear in other sections of the Canvas. That is alright. All boxes are linked, and over time, content in one box will move to another. The overall goal is for you to identify what is missing and link it to what you are planning, or should plan, to do.

Desired Outcome

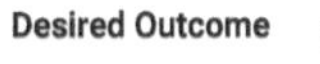

At the bottom end of the Canvas is one of its most important parts, besides the actual problems you identify.

This is the space where you express what you are expect, not only from this strategic policy analysis exercise, but from your overall approach to AI regulation. More concretely, from having an AI Regulatory Policy that improves AI regulations and, therefore, AI results in your country.

How to Use Your BRAIn Canvas

The Canvas is a visual, high-level, strategic tool. Feel free to use it flexibly regarding where, how and with whom. Again, the important elements are the collaboration, discussions and ideas that will emerge as you start filling its different sections.

Nonetheless, here are a few suggestions to guide your use of the Canvas:

- **Be inclusive.** The BRAIn Canvas is not only for one brain It works best when several people are involved in creating it. So, be inclusive.

- **Let people understand it first.** I have been in workshops or meetings where the facilitator assigns a task on the spot, and gives the participants 5–10 minutes to discuss and solve everything. Do not do that. Give people enough time to get familiar with the BRAIn Canvas before asking them to jump straight into it.

- **Create options for multiple inputs.** If you are running a live workshop or meeting, print out the canvas or set up large pieces of paper, cardboard or wall sections with each part of the BRAIn Canvas. Team members should add their inputs using Post-it notes or by writing directly. If you prefer or need online collaboration, use tools that allow different people to add their views. Offline or online, the goal is to use the Canvas to bring together different perspectives to discuss, ideate and create a shared strategic vision that can lead the way forward.

- **Create the necessary space and time to work on the Canvas.** Do not work on the Canvas on a busy day or time. Good thinking and discussions emerge when people have time to think and be present, not when they have thousands of other things to do or pay attention to. You know your team better, so create that space and find the time when they can shine.

- **Reach out.** I will be happy to support you and your team if you need help. I have created an online version of the BRAIn Canvas to help agency teams brainstorm and collaborate in a simple and interactive way. The ultimate goal is to facilitate your process of developing a strategy and roadmap for an AI Regulatory Policy. Other experts can also support you using the Canvas.

Key messages to remember

- The BRAIn Canvas is a visual tool to help you map and put together many of the things covered in the book, from a high-level, strategic perspective.
- When using it, a very important part is the collaboration, discussions and ideas it can create within your teams. Use the Canvas with that in mind.
- As a leader, make sure you have a good enough environment and conditions for you and your teams to get the most out of this tool.
- I created an online version of the BRAIn Canvas to support you. Feel free to reach out if you need help. Or scan the QR code below to download a PDF version available on my personal website.

It Goes Beyond AI Regulation

Part 4 has one final chapter, in which I want to share something that goes beyond the technical aspects of better AI regulations. This chapter will focus on the most important change this agenda needs.

After this part, I will conclude with a summary of key takeaways and a call-to-action.

11

Better People, Better AI Results

"Everyone thinks of changing the world, but no one thinks of changing himself."

—Leo Tolstoy

"The world as we have created it is a process of our thinking. It cannot be changed without changing our thinking."

—Albert Einstein

If you made it to this final chapter, I am sure you are a leader—current or future—who believes that things can be different. That transformation is possible, even when everyone thinks the opposite and settles for the "this-is-how-things-work" idea of leadership.

I am also pretty sure that, despite your excitement and enthusiasm, you realize that this agenda to improve AI regulations and achieve better AI results is quite a challenge.

Indeed, it is a big challenge. That is why I want to give you honest advice. A reality check.

It is very likely that, as good, talented, motivated, and determined as you are, you will not get everything right. You will not fix everything that is wrong with how your government approaches and handles AI regulation.

This is an important recognition to make. There are so many pieces, actors and situations that are not under your control, even when you are in the driver's seat and commanding a team, department, agency, organization or country.

As difficult as this recognition is, it is your way out, your way to create space, acquire freedom and focus on the only thing you can really change: You.

The beauty of being a leader does not come from having followers or from telling others what to do, including orders for them to change. You should know that is not leadership. That is popularity and authority.

The real beauty of leadership is that you can influence positive change and transformation by setting an example. By showing that you have changed yourself and act differently.

Of course, when leading this agenda, there will be plenty of moments when changing yourself may not seem enough. Remember, that is the only thing you can control. Your transformation is the best you can offer.

Let's talk briefly in this chapter about a few things you might consider when trying to bring transformation through AI regulation by changing yourself.

Your Deep Motivations

When I went to Georgetown to study public policy, I heard someone say that compared to MBA students, who often aim for money, public policy students aim to do good. Deep into my professional career, I still have that feeling.

You have your reasons for buying and reading this book. Whether it was intellectual or professional interest, because you love reading, or something else, as an author, I really appreciate you doing it.

If your initial motivation was to get on this bandwagon of AI and ride the tide while trying not to be left behind, my kudos to you. That can be a way to start meaningful things, too.

I hope that, in return, this book added a little extra to that initial motivation and planted the idea that aiming for better AI regulation is an opportunity to bring positive change and transformation.

If that feeling sank deeper through your core—or if it was already there when you decided to buy and read this book—do not forget about it. Even when things seem to be going well, and especially when they are not.

Keep coming back to that motivation, just as meditation helps a distracted mind come back to the present, the only thing that we have, the only place to change the past, future and the present itself.

My motivations for writing this book are simple. I enjoy sharing knowledge and ideas, and I enjoy writing. There is a lot of freedom that comes from doing it when it is just you and a piece of paper. Deeper still, I believe positive change is possible.

I guess having a black piece of paper, as an author, is a similar situation to when someone drafts a new regulation, a new AI regulation. But beyond intention, the mindset and approach to the task also matter.

Regulatory Humility

The concept of regulatory humility came to me a few years after I had advised, or had witnessed and supported how other colleagues advised, governments on the "how" to regulate.

My thinking on this idea was cemented when talking and working with regulators in several countries about changes to their "what."

When you google "regulatory humility," you'll find different meanings and interpretations. However, my views on this concept come from a very common practice followed by governments worldwide when they decide to regulate: *regulatory decisions are usually set and fixed from the first minute, with little space for adjustment or reconsideration afterward.*

Whatever comes next in the "how" to formalize that decision is often just a "dance" to justify what has already been decided while pretending there is transparency, public consultations, use of evidence and other "positive" qualities in the decision-making process.

In other words, many times governments know what they want, and they do not always mind what others have to say—even within government. They believe they know their "business"—that is why they are the government—and they do not care much about evidence or questioning their initial ideas. That would be seen as a sign of "weakness."

Of course, I have worked with great regulators and teams that act very differently. But the "I have all the answers" mindset is not rare across the globe. Some may say it is how governments work. It is part of their DNA.

The good news is that you, as a leader, are not your government. You have the choice—even if you think it may be political suicide—to think and act differently. To change the mindset you bring into the space of AI regulation. That new mindset is what I call "regulatory humility."

If you embrace my version of regulatory humility, it means leaving behind the idea that you, as a leader, hold all the answers to everything your government or organization must address. This is critically important for AI and AI regulation, where there are many unknowns and constantly evolving challenges.

Regulatory humility also means that this initial recognition is your way out. Your doorway to seek collaboration, inputs and help from others.

It is an important step to take, and then move forward without fear or insecurity, grounded in the confidence that big issues take more than a village to resolve.

This should lead you to talk more with the rest of your team, across government, and with the private sector, experts and others. If you decide to take this approach, do it with a curious mind and open ears. By doing this, you gain knowledge and respect from those you listen to.

It is probably not the prototypical recipe to advance a career in a leadership group dominated by politics and a bureaucratic mindset. However, it is what you have to do if you accept what I said about your individual limitations to fix everything that is wrong in your government's approach to AI regulation, so you can focus on changing the only thing you can really change: yourself, including your regulatory mindset and decision-making.

I will conclude this section by returning to another concept I have mentioned several times throughout the book that is also related to regulatory humility: procedural fairness.

Remember when, in Chapter 6, I said:

"When people perceive that decisions are made following a fair process, they are more likely to accept those decisions, even if they do not agree with them."

In that chapter, I also mentioned that to improve the perception of a fair process in decision-making, people affected by those decisions need to perceive that four things are happening:

- Having a voice in the matters or decisions that are affecting them;
- Being treated with respect and dignity by those making decisions;
- Receiving explanations about final decisions and outcomes; and
- Knowing that the decision-maker is transparent, neutral and has trustworthy motives.

Procedural fairness is a key component of a regulatory humility mindset. If you want to make changes and truly lead the agenda of AI regulation in your government, agency, department or team, this is part of the transformation you need to undergo first.

My wish at this point is for you to realize that this change depends on only one thing: You.

Positive Coordination

This is a subset of the regulatory humility mindset, but because coordination is so fundamental to getting AI regulation and your AI Regulatory Policy right—as discussed in Chapter 9—I am dedicating a few separate lines to it.

I invite you to read "The Challenge of Policy Coordination" by Guy Peters, Professor or American Government at the University of Pittsburgh. It is a short paper that complements Chapter 9 very well.

From his paper, I want to highlight the idea that governments should not only care about coordination because they want to prevent conflicting, duplicative, or contradictory decisions. Of course, that matters a lot in general and in AI regulation.

However, Peters contrasts "negative coordination," which is an attempt to avoid conflicting and inconsistent decisions, with the concept of "positive coordination."

By positive coordination, he means:[48]

"Positive coordination, however, would require the organizations to go beyond simply avoiding conflicts and to seek to find ways to cooperate on solutions that can benefit all the organizations involved, and their clients."

In his paper, he then explains some of the reasons organizations fail to coordinate or resist doing more of it. Some of these you know from experience, and I have mentioned them throughout the book. Nonetheless, here is a short list: silos, power, politics, turf, ideologies and preconceptions.

Many of these things are not under your control. In fact, many have been fed into your government leader's mindset or the *software in our mind,* just as my friend and first boss ever, Felipe Gonzalez y Gonzalez, used to teach at IPADE.

Part of your job is to uninstall that software, so you gain space and freedom to make different choices. The choices that not everyone can make, and choices that better AI regulation and the world need.

Better You, Better AI Results

When I was at the IDB, I created a slogan for our team: "Better Regulations, Better Results." My goal was to communicate that governments can achieve better policy results by improving their regulations.

Of course, the chain does not stop there. As I mentioned a couple of times in the book, Cesar Cordova says that you cannot have better regulations without better regulators.

I will take a step forward and add another link to that chain by saying that you cannot have better regulators without better people.

On the surface, you may think that better people mean having teams and staff that know more about the "how," "what," "who," and "why" of AI regulation. Yes, that knowledge and those technical skills are important for your teams and government to have.

But, as the name of Part 4 says, it goes beyond AI regulation. People deliver better results, and live their best selves, when they are motivated, when they have space to think, and when they find meaning in what they do.

I hope it is clear by now that there are many things you cannot, and should not, aim to control about the people behind AI regulation and the people under your command as a government leader, and that the only thing you can control and change is you.

Find the best version of yourself. Once you are in that position, you may help others do the same.

Although in this final chapter I have hinted at a few things you could change about your mindset as a leader, my book is not about how you can become a better you. That is an individual journey we all need to walk, yes, with support from others, but mainly on our own.

If you find it difficult to change yourself, start by embracing this agenda. Along the journey, I am pretty sure it will change you.

As you continue walking this path, I wish you the best and I want to leave you with one final thought: a better you is where the chain starts, the chain that leads to better AI results.

Now What?

"You can't go back and change the beginning, but you can start where you are and change the ending."

—Attributed to C.S. Lewis

Some of the books I have enjoyed the most are those that leave you with messages you remember and that motivate you to view, or do, things differently afterward. I do hope my book left you with a little bit of both.

Because many things are forgotten after reading a book, and with the passage of time, I will close with a summary that complements the sections with "key messages to remember" sections I left at the end of each chapter.

- This book is not about this or that AI regulation. I hope by now you understand why.
- This book is for you, a current or future government or organization leader, who wants not only to get better results from AI through better AI regulations, but also to bring positive transformation along the process.
- One of your first tasks is to learn to regulate better. That is the real pacing problem many governments are facing.

- When regulation is represented as something that only stifles innovation, remember that regulation also serves other purposes, like pro
tecting desirable public goods.
- The principles and essence of sound regulatory policy are a solid foundation for your government to develop its own AI Regulatory Policy that improves the "how" you regulate AI and the outcomes you can get from it.
- Actively managing the lifecycle of your AI regulation will not only increase its likelihood of success but will also set the tone for future compliance and rebuilding trust in your government.
- When you get to the "what" to regulate about AI, you will have to balance two goals that may conflict with each other: promoting AI's growth and protecting everyone from the consequences and irresponsible use of AI.
- At some point, AI can help you better regulate AI and other policy domains. That is one of the things I aim for with my GovTech startup, fAIrly simple. You should also explore this idea.
- Although regulating AI through the lens of your AI Regulatory Policy should be simple and straightforward, it does not mean it will be easy in practice. This policy faces many challenges and "killers" that can send good intentions to the grave, as in any bureaucracy.
- If putting together everything needed for your government to succeed with AI regulation becomes daunting, remember you can use the BRAIn Canvas in Chapter 10. I created an online collaborative version to help your agencies and teams use this tool more effectively. You can download a PDF version at https://alfredogb.com/book or using the QR Code at the end of Chapter 10.

- As you face these challenges, you will realize that there are many things you cannot control, and hopefully, you now understand that you should not aim to control them.
- The only change you can control is your personal change.
- This agenda requires you to change, to be a different leader, a better you, with a different mindset and ways of doing things.
- If at some point you find it difficult to change yourself, start by embracing this agenda. It will change you along the way.

So, now what? I guess it depends on where you are. If you are a future leader, keep building on these and other ideas that will help you act differently when your time comes. If you are already a leader, whether at the top of your team, unit, department, ministry, organization, government or country, this is your time.

If you feel inspired to do something different about AI regulation, I hope you realize that you just have to do it, especially the things within your control or worth fighting for.

There are no guarantees it will be easy. Nothing that matters in life is easy. Acting differently is difficult because it demands that we change. But this is not something you just need to be told. You need to discover it for yourself.

When you decide to do something different to improve your AI regulations, I would like to hear about it. Send me an email at alfredo@AlfredoGB.com And if I can help or advise you, I will be happy to do it.

Acknowledgments

I would like to start by thanking all the people who, directly or indirectly, intentionally or without even noticing, have influenced me as a person and author. They include my family, friends, teachers, colleagues, authors I have read, government clients and even people with whom I had random conversations or encounters and never saw again. My wish is that I have also given you something in return.

A key catalyst behind this book was my dearest friend, Dani Alvarez. I talked to you about this book when it was only an idea. Your words of encouragement and support gave me the gentle push I needed to make it something real. Beyond that nudge, I deeply appreciate, treasure and enjoy our friendship.

The course I took at Harvard on "Data Science and Artificial Intelligence: Ethics, Governance, and Laws," with Prof. Bruce Huang, was very important in deciding to focus this book on AI regulation. Regulating AI is going to be one of the most challenging and important responsibilities governments will face in the years to come. Thank you, Prof. Huang, for encouraging me to develop the ideas that started as a very rough policy note.

Professionally, it is rare to find someone who also sees things that you see and others don't. Thank you, Bryan O'Byrne, for the exchanges we have had about GRP and other topics around regulation, whether over coffee or a few paddles. I appreciate that you took the time to review my manuscript.

Thank you also, Peter Ladegaard, for your feedback on the manuscript. I also deeply appreciate our work together. It was not only my entry point to the world of better regulation, but also a time when I discovered—with your guidance, and sometimes without it—that I was able to combine thinking with doing.

I have worked with other great people, so it is unfair not to mention and thank all of them. However, I want to recognize someone special: my first boss ever, Felipe Gonzalez y Gonzalez. You are wise and a great human. I admire you, and I learned so much from our time together at IPADE. It was a delight and a pleasure to hear your lectures. Your views on things, people, and life have stayed with me for years.

Along the journey, my writing has been influenced by colleagues and authors I have read. I would like to thank: Agustin Llamas (RIP) and the initial training I got at IPADE Business School; Keith McLean, Peter Ladegaard and other colleagues at the World Bank, from whom I learned how to be direct and assertive; communications colleagues for their advice on how to better connect with non-expert audiences; my time at Georgetown University, where I discovered a very important thing about writing—that I have something to say, and that it matters; my years at Universidad Panamericana in Mexico, because as an engineer I did not develop my writing skills, but I gain a lot in human values and perspective; and finally the many authors who helped me realize that it is not enough to have a voice and use it, but that when that voice connects with what it is inside, you deliver your best, which made writing this book a lot easier than I initially thought.

I would also like to thank the team at The Publishing Pad. It is not easy to be a first-time author. Thank you, Chisom Ezeh, Chioma Noble-Anyahuru, Aistis Samulionis, and Ayo Adeshina for all your help and guidance that took this book from a manuscript to a successful launch.

Finally, I want to thank my wife, Mariana, and daughter, Sofia. Mariana, you have always been there supporting my dreams and passions. Thank you for being my Editor in Chief and reading everything I want to publish. Thank you especially for your love and for being there in the good and the bad. I admire you as a woman, wife and mother. Sofia, you are everything I could ever ask for. I still remember when I told you I was going to write a book and you asked with a mix of surprise and emotion, "You're going to be an author?" I hope you realize that if an engineer and numbers guy like me can write a book, then anything in life is possible. :)

About Me

Alfredo González Briseño is a leading policy innovator and expert specializing in the governance of regulation for the age of Artificial Intelligence. Drawing on his years advising governments on business environment reforms at multilateral development banks, including the World Bank, Alfredo focuses on the "how" of regulation—designing efficient, clear and predictable legal frameworks.

He is the founder of the GovTech startup fAIrly simple, which uses AI to make regulations clear, accessible and smarter. With a career spanning Washington D.C. and his upbringing in Mexico, he offers a unique global perspective that connects high-level policy discussions with the practical regulatory challenges faced by emerging economies.

He also authors the responsible AI publication fAIr and square on Medium. Visit https://medium.com/@alfredogb to read more of his works.

Scan this QR code to learn more about Alfredo, his actionable resources, strategic advisory services, speaking opportunities and content or just visit https://AlfredoGB.com.

About fAIrly simple

fAIrly simple is a GovTech startup that uses AI to deliver clear, accessible and smarter regulations. From Northern Virginia, we serve and advise governments, the private sector and organizations worldwide that struggle with regulatory complexity.

Regulations clear, accessible and smarter

Learn more about us by scanning this QR code or visiting https://fairlysimple.io/

If you are curious about what you read in **Chapter 7 "Use AI to Create Better AI Regulation,"** or are ready to start using AI to improve regulations in your country or organization, reach out via email at contactus@fairlysimple.io

References

Ahmad, R. (2024, March 4). Engineers often need a lot of water to keep data centers cool. In Water Works, Civil Engineering Source. American Society of Civil Engineers.

Aladesanmi, A. (2023, May 1). Agile Regulation and the Future of Governance. *The Regulatory Review*, PPR News, Penn Program on Regulation. University of Pennsylvania.

Blair, T. (2024). *On Leadership: Lessons for the 21st Century*. Crown.

Bredbenner, M. (2024, June 2). Risk-Based Regulatory Regimes. (P. P. Regulation, Ed.) *The Regulatory Review*.

Burke, J. K. S. (2023). Procedural Fairness. Presentation. Berkeley Judicial Institute.

Choo, L. (2024, October 4). How 2 Students Used The Meta Ray-Bans To Access Personal Information. *Forbes*.

CIPL (2023). Ten Recommendations for Global AI Regulation. Washington, DC: Center for Information Policy Leadership.

Copley, M. (2022, August 30). Data centers, backbone of the digital economy, face water scarcity and climate risk. NPR.

Desjardins, D. (2024, March 5). Summary: Discussing Agile Regulation. Regulatory Studies Center, George Washington University.

DOE. (2024, December 20). DOE Releases New Report Evaluating Increase in Electricity Demand from Data Centers. Press release about the publication of the "2024 Report on U.S. Data Center Energy Use," by the Lawrence Berkeley National Laboratory. U.S. Department of Energy.

González Briseño, A. 2020. Fighting Regulatory Surprises Online: Practical considerations for participatory rulemaking through online public consultation. Unpublished draft.

González Briseño, A. (2024, May 6). ¿Cómo evitar que la regulación mate a la innovación? Revista ISTMO, pp. 28–32.

Habuka, H. (2003, February 14). Japan's Approach to AI Regulation and Its Impact on the 2023 G7 Presidency. Center for Strategic & International Studies (CSIS).

Hartmann, E. (2024, July 5). How smart speakers can compromise your privacy. Retrieved from Moxso.

Hicken, A., Malesky, E., Nillasithanukroh, S., and Taussig, M. (2023). Digital consultation of firms and perception of government's regulatory legitimacy: Piloting an experiment in regulation design in Thailand. London: International Growth Center.

IEA. (2025, April 10). AI is set to drive surging electricity demand from data centres while offering the potential to transform how the energy sector works. Press release about IEA's special report "Energy and AI." International Energy Agency.

Johnson, W. G. (2023). Caught in quicksand? Compliance and legitimacy challenges in using regulatory sandboxes to manage emerging technologies. *Regulation and Governance, 17,* pp. 709–725.

Lind, E. and Arndt, C. (2016). Perceived Fairness and Regulatory Policy: A Behavioural Science Perspective on Government-Citizen Interactions. *OECD Regulatory Policy Working Papers,* No. 6, OECD Publishing, Paris.

Lind, E. and Arndt, C. (2018). Creating Trusted Regulatory Policy. *The Regulatory Review.* Penn Program on Regulation. University of Pennsylvania.

Loayza N. and Woolcock M. (2020, March 5). Designing good policies is one thing, implementing them is another. Let's Talk Development blog. The World Bank Group.

Malesky, E., and Taussig, M. (2019). Participation, Government Legitimacy, and Regulatory Compliance in Emerging Economies: A Firm-Level Field Experiment in Vietnam. *American Political Science Review,* 113(2), pp. 530–551.

Ng, C., & Prestes, E. (2023, November 14). It's time we embrace an agile approach to regulating AI. Emerging Technologies, World Economic Forum.

North, Douglass C. (1990). *Institutions, Institutional Change and Economic Performance.* Cambridge University Press.

OECD (2008). *Measuring Regulatory Quality.* OECD Policy Brief, April 2008.

OECD (2019). *Better Regulation Practices across the European Union.* OECD Publishing, Paris.

OECD (2020). *Regulatory Impact Assessment, OECD Best Practice Principles for Regulatory Policy.* Paris: OECD Publishing.

OECD, C. f. (2021, October 6). *Recommendation of the Council for Agile Regulatory Governance to Harness Innovation.* OECD Legal Instruments, Organization for Economic Co-operation and Development.

OECD (2023). Regulatory sandboxes in artificial intelligence. *OECD Digital Economy Papers,* No. 356, OECD Publishing, Paris.

Oxford Economics. (2025, May 27). Educated but unemployed, a rising reality for US college grads. Research Briefing. Oxford Economics Group.

Peters, B. G. (2018). The challenge of policy coordination. *Policy Design and Practice,* 1(1), pp. 1–11.

Pinheiro Privette, A. (2024, October 11). AI's Challenging Waters. Article from the Center for Secure Water (C4SW), published in the news section of The Grainer College of Engineering, University of Illinois Urbana-Champaign.

Roose, K. (2025, June 20). For Some Recent Graduates, the A.I. Job Apocalypse May Already Be Here. The New York Times.

SELC (2025, January 10). Data centers are a hot topic for Virginia legislators. News article by the Southern Environmental Law Center.

Sharma, L. (2024, December 19). AI Data Centers Threaten Global Water Security. Cybersecurity & Tech and Foreign Relations & International Law. The Lawfare Institute.

Slijkerman, J. F. (2024, April 24). Data is the new gold for AI development. ING THINK.

SPN (2021, October 12). Everything you need to know about regulatory sandboxes. State Policy Network.

Stackpole, B. (2025, January 7). AI has high data center energy costs — but there are solutions. Ideas Made to Matter – Sustainability; MIT Sloan School of Management.

The UK Government. (2023, August 3). A pro-innovation approach to AI regulation. Policy Paper by the Department of Science, Innovation and Technology, Office of Artificial Intelligence.

Thierer, A. (2018, August 8). The Pacing Problem and the Future of Technology Regulation: Why Policymakers Must Adapt to a World That's Constantly Innovating. Technology and Innovation, Expert Commentary, Mercatus Center, George Mason University.

Van Rooij, B., and Fine, A. (2021). The Behavioral Code: The Hidden Ways that Law Makes us Better… or Worse. Beacon Press.

Witter, L. and Samant, J. (2020, January 31). These 10 tips for tech regulators will drive innovation. Geo-Economics and Politics article. World Economic Forum.

World Bank Group (2020). Global Investment Competitiveness Report 2019/2020: Rebuilding Investor Confidence in Times of Uncertainty. Washington, DC: World Bank.

WEF (2024). Fintech has outgrown sandboxes. Now it needs airports. By Dante Disparte. World Economic Forum Story. September 27, 2024.

WEF (2025). Future of Jobs 2025 Insight Report. World Economic Forum.

Yale Law School. (NA). Procedural Justice. The Justice ColLaboratory.

Endnotes

1   For more details, see: Thierer, 2018.

2   For more details, see: Witter and Samant, 2020.

3   For more details, see: Ng & Prestes, 2023; Aladesanmi, 2023; Desjardins, 2024; and OECD C. f., 2021.

4   For more details, see: OECD C. f., 2021.

5   For more details, see: the UK Government, 2023.

6   For more details, see: North, 1990.

7   Ibid.

8   For more details, see: Van Rooij and Fine, 2021.

9   For more details, see: OECD, 2008.

10   For more details, see: OECD, 2019.

11   For more details, see: Lind and Arndt, 2016 and 2018.

12   For more details, see: World Bank, 2020.

13   To learn more about this Policy, please see https://www.canada.ca/en/government/system/laws/developing-improving-federal-regulations/requirements-developing-managing-reviewing-regulations/guidelines-tools/policy-regulatory-transparency-accountability.html#toc7.

14   For more details, see: Pichai, S. (2023, May 23). Opinion Artificial Intelligence.

15   For more details, see: OECD, 2020.

16   For more details, see: Lind and Arndt, 2016.

17   Ibid.

18   For more details, see: González Briseño, 2020.

19   For more details, see: Lind and Arndt, 2016.

20   For more details, see: Malesky and Taussig, 2019; and Hicken, Malesky, Nillasithanukroh, and Taussig, 2023.

21   For more details, see: Habuka, 2023.

22   For more details, see: Stackpole, 2025.

23   For more details, see: World Bank, 2020.

24   For more details, see: SPN, 2021.

25   For more details, see: González Briseño, 2024.

26   For more details, see: Johnson, 2023.

27   For more details, see: OECD, 2023.

28   For more details, see: CIPL, 2023.

29   For more details, see: Bredbenner, 2024.

30   For more details, see: Habuka, 2023.

31   For more details, see: Slijkerman, 2024.

32   For more details, see: Hartmann, 2024.

33   For more details, see: Choo, 2024.

34   For more details, see: Lind and Arndt, 2016; Yale, NA.; and Burke (2023).

35   For more details, see: IEA, 2025.

36   For more details, see: DOE, 2024.

37   For more details, see: Stackpole, 2025.

38   For more details, see: Sharma, 2024.

39   For more details, see: Copley, 2022.

40   For more details, see: Pinheiro Privette, 2024.

41   For more details, see: SELC, 2025.

42   For more details, see: Ahmad, 2024.

43   For more details, see: WEF, 2025.

44   For more details, see: Oxford Economics, 2025.

45   For more details, see: Roose, 2025.

46   For more details, see: Loayza and Woolcock, 2020.

47   For more details, see and read Blair, 2024.

48   For more details, see Peters, 2018.